THE
HEALING
GARDEN

THE HEALING GARDEN

Natural Healing for Mind, Body and Soul

DAVID SQUIRE

vega

ISBN   1–84333–584–0

A catalogue record for this book is available from the British Library

Published in 2002 by
Vega
64 Brewery Road
London, N7 9NT

A member of the Chrysalis Group plc
Visit our website at www.chrysalisbooks.co.uk

Printed and bound in Spain

Half-title page: A paradise garden is revealed in this 1770 painting of an Indian garden in Hyderabad. The birds and animals, together with the musical pipes, introduce vibrancy to the garden.
Frontispiece: The Chinese consider that old trees are of benefit in the garden as they attract and harbour beneficial *chi* (energy).
Above: The sound of splashing water has a repetitive but irregular nature that introduces a comforting and healing quality to gardens.

PICTURE CREDITS

The publisher would like to thank the following agencies and individuals for providing the illustrations used in this book:

British Library: page 130; **Peter Clayton:** page 19 (tl); **Colour Library Books, International:** pages 16 (all), 20 (all), 29 (all), 31(b), 39, 69, 70 (all r), 74 (l&r), 86 (all), 113 (all), 115 (all), 119 (r), 126, 129 (b), 132 (t), 133 (t & b), 134, 136 (tl), 137 (t); **David Squire:** pages 8 (r), 9 (r), 10 (1), 13 (tr), 19 (tr), 20 (tl), 65, 99 (t), 100 (1), 104 (1), 106 (b), 108 (1), 109 (t), 117; **Efamol Evening Primrose Oil:** page 78 (t); **E.T, Archive:** pages 9 (b), 139 (b); **Biblioteca Estense, Madrid:** page 6; **Bibliothèque Nationale, Paris:** pages 102, 105 (b); **British Museum:** pages 10 (r), 11; **Buonconsiglio Castle Trento:** page 105 (t); **Jeremy Thomas:** front cover; **Marco Polo Gallery, Paris:** frontispiece, page 124; **Musée des Beaux Arts, Lille:** page 21; **Prado Madrid:** page 40; **Stadelisches Kunstinstitut:** page 12 (t); **Victoria & Albert Museum, London:** pages 13 (tl), 104 (r); **John Glover:** pages 7, 8 (r), 14, 22 (all), 23, 25, 30 (all), 31, 34 (both b), 35, 36 (t), 38, 41 (l), 42, 44, 46, 47, 48 (all b), 49, 51(b), 53 (b), 54, 56 (t), 57, 58, 59, 60, 61(t), 64, 66, 67, 68, 71(1), 72 (r) 73 (1), 76, 77, 78 (b), 79, 80 (t), 81, 82 (b), 84 (b), 85 (t), 87, 88, 89, 90 (r), 91(b), 92, 93, 9498 (r), 100 (r), 101 (b), 108 (m), 109 (1), 111 (1), 112 (r), 114, 118 (b). 120 (t), 121, 122 (1), 123, 132, 135, 137 (bl), 138 (b); **Vana Haggerty:** (illustrations) pages 12 (1), 17 (tr), 18 (1), 24 (1), 26 (t), 27 (both r), 30 (t), 31(r), 32 (t), 36 (b), 41 (right), 42 (1), 43, 48 (tl), 50 (1), 52 (t), 70 (1), 71(r), 72 (1), 73 (r), 75, 80 (t), 84 (1), 85 (r), 87 (br), 90 (1), 98 (1), 101 (r), 106 (t), 107 (r), 108 (r), ill (r), 112 (1), 125, 129 (t), 132 (1), 136 (t), 137 (br), 138 (r), 139 (tl); **Jerry Harpur:** page 97 (t); **Holt Studios International:** pages 15, 24 (1), 26 (b), 27 (b), 95, 103, 131; **Israeli Tourist Board:** page 18 (b); **Life File:** pages 13 (b), 37 (b) (Gina Green), 30 (Nicola Sutton); **Lindley Library, Royal Horticultural Society:** pages 45, 55, 56 (b), 61(b), 110, 128, 136 (b); **Nature Photographers:** pages 96 (Frank Blackburn), 120 (b) (Geoff Du Feu), 120 (b), 28 (Paul Sterry); **Peter Newark's Historical Pictures:** page 122 (r); **David Squire:** 17 (tl & b), 19 (b), 35, 37 (t), 41(r), 48 (tr), 50 (b), 51 (tr), 53 (t), 66 (b), 82 (t), 83 (t), 97 (b), 107 (1), 116, 119 (b); **Catriona Tudor-Erler:** pages 33, 52 (b), 62, 63, 74 (m), 118 (t), 127

CONTENTS

INTRODUCTION

The Hebrew poet who wrote the Book of Genesis in the Judaic Bible told that life began in a garden, and that the Garden of Eden provided 'every tree that is pleasant to the sight and good for food'. According to Genesis, out of Eden rivers flowed to the four corners of the world.

The concept of Eden as a garden is part of many religions; the Koran mentions Gardens of Eden, 'underneath which rivers flow, forever therein to dwell'. Indeed, the idea of a garden as paradise is part of Persian culture and dates back to 6000 BC. The Garden of Eden is thought to have been in Mesopotamia, an ancient country in Asia between the rivers Tigris and Euphrates, and at one time part of the Persian Empire, now Iran.

In almost every nation of antiquity there was a Garden of Paradise, with plants held sacred for their spiritual or healing powers. The curative nature of some plants often gave them religious status, especially at a time when in some religions disease was believed to be divine retribution for personal sins. Plants thought to have religious qualities were mainly trees, as their longevity provided historical status and continuity from one season to another. However, *Ocimum tenuifolium* is a herbaceous and woody plant widely known as Holy Basil,

Sacred Basil or Tulsi and is sacred to the Hindus; at one time it was found in nearly every Hindu house throughout India. Earlier, it was aptly known as *Ocimum sanctum.* Of quite a different nature, *Nelumbo nucifera,* the Sacred Lotus or Nelumbo, is a water plant which was revered by Egyptians from early times, as well as venerated in parts of India, Burma, Sri Lanka and China.

The Sacred Fig, *Ficus religiosa,* which also answers to the Bo Tree, or Peepul, is perhaps the most revered tree of India and Sri Lanka, venerated by both Buddhists and Hindus.

In South America in the 1830s, the naturalist Charles Darwin told of a

sacred tree on the Rio Negro, writing: 'We came in sight of a famous tree which the Indians reverence as the altar of Walleechu.' In North America, totem-clans were often named after trees and plants, and each member of the clan was believed to have descended from a particular plant.

In England, trees such as the oak and thorn have had religious significance in pagan traditions and early Christian lore. The oak is connected to the gods Zeus, Hercules, Janus and Thor. The word Druid translates as 'oak-man'. Their annual sacrifice involved an oak bough. The famous Glastonbury Thorn – which blossoms, almost miraculously, at Christmastime – is said to have grown from Joseph of Arimathea's staff, which he pushed into the ground when he first arrived in Glastonbury. Thorn trees were important markers of territory in Celtic countries, and towns such as Thornton and Thornsett still reflect that ancient association in their names.

Facing page: In a beautiful garden, Venus, the goddess of beauty and love, offers a chalice of water from the fountain of eternal youth in the fifteenth-century manuscript *Madena de Sphaera.*

Centre: The fragrant sacred lotus, *Nelumbo nucifera,* is revered by Hindus and Buddhists. The roots can be eaten as a vegetable or ground to form lotus meal, which is rich in starch.

MOVING TREES

The Egyptians developed techniques for transplanting large trees. First a trench was dug around the tree, then the workers cut the soil directly under the tree to unearth a large soil-covered root ball.

The soil-ball was held together and kept moist by wrapping it in cloth, then transported in a wickerwork basket suspended on poles and carried by slaves.

Right: The ancient Egyptians frequently decorated their temples with hieroglyphics depicting plants and the cultivation of land.

NEANDERTHAL MAN

Indications of early agriculture date back only 10,000 years, although it is certain that an appreciation of the beauty and comforting nature of flowers goes back longer. Examination of Neanderthal burial sites from about 60,000 years ago indicate that cornflowers, yarrow, grape hyacinths and other flowers were placed around dead bodies.

Natural 'gardens' in forest clearings or along riverbanks must have created areas of rest and pleasure for early men and women, perhaps inspiring the plants' association with the gods and spirits of the natural world.

EARLY GARDENS

The creation of ornamental gardens indicates a degree of civilization and a settled economy. The first cultures to move from a hunter-gatherers economy, where food was collected as available seasonally, to a settled agrarian way of life, were in the 'fertile crescent' of the Middle East, between the valleys of the rivers Euphrates and Tigris, the Persian Gulf and the Mediterranean sea.

The Sumerians, who became established in southern Mesopotamia by about 3000 BC, are believed to have come from the forests of Armenia to the north. They built mounds or platforms and planted them with trees, supposedly to provide new homes for the forest gods. Apart from these venerated trees, we know little of what Sumerian and Assyrian gardens were like, although

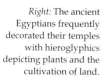

carvings indicate vines and several kinds of tree, but not flowers. The earliest evidence of an actual garden appears in Egyptian tomb paintings. In 1549 BC, Queen Hatshepsut sent a plant-gathering expedition to the Land of Punt (thought to be Somalia) to bring back incense trees for planting on terraced gardens of the mortuary temple she built for herself near Thebes.

Paintings and the contents of tombs indicate that the Egyptians grew corn pop pies, convolvulus, mallow and many other flowers, as well as culinary and medicinal plants. Figs, date palms, lilies, pomegranates and vines were also cultivated by them.

The Hanging Gardens of Babylon

These famous gardens are reputed to have been built by King Nebuchadnezzar (604–562 BC) for his Persian wife, Mayitis, who was homesick for her native country. The late first-century Greek historian Diodorus Siculus tells a different story. His writings state that the gardens were constructed by Cyrus, a Persian king who ruled around 500 BC, to please a courtesan. Whatever the truth, the gardens seem to have been built to please a woman, and are still considered one of the wonders of the ancient world.

The Persians loved gardens and flowers. When the Persians invaded and conquered Assyria, Babylon and Egypt, they introduced not only their laws and customs but also their gardens. The Persian style was adapted to suit the climate of each country. It is said that when Xerxes I, a Persian king who ruled around 500 BC, was on his way to conquer Greece, he came across a particularly attractive tree. He ordered guards to protect it, and had its branches arrayed in golden chains.

Greeks and Romans

Early Greeks were shepherds and farmers, rather than gardeners, but they did gather the wild flowers that smothered

GOD OF NATURE

For many centuries, early man called upon the gods to help gain greater fertility for land and to identify with nature. The ancient Egyptians did this through Mut, the God of Nature.

Left: As early as 1200 BC the Egyptians decorated the walls of their tombs. This painting from the tomb of Sennudem (nineteenth dynasty) shows a man ploughing with oxen and a woman scattering seed.

MAGICAL HOLLY

Holly was thought to protect against evil spirits, poison and lightning. In fact the leaves act like miniature lightning conductors, giving the trees immunity. The Bach flower remedies use holly to treat oversensitivity, hatred and aggressive behaviour.

Right The North American village of Secoton (later known as Secota) was sketched by Captain John White, leader of the first expeditions to what he called New England. His sketch shows corn in three stages of growth. Later, when the German engraver Theodor de Bry came to engrave the scene for publication, he added sunflowers, pumpkins and tobacco.

Facing page: The Muslim Prophet Ali Husein and Hasan in Paradise (from the *Khavarannameh,* 1686. Persian gardens have inspired garden designers since Alexander the Great's armies brought back new plants and ideas from his conquests in that region.

the hillsides in spring to use in garlands for religious festivals. Later, they were grown by professional nurserymen who sold them to garland-makers. Greek gardens were practical rather than ornamental; mainly fruit and vines were grown.

In about 350 BC, Alexander the Great and his armies returned from Egypt and Persia with tales of an amazing wealth of plants. They introduced new plants and ideas into Greek colonies; Alexandria, a city on the Nile delta, was extravagantly designed, with more than a quarter of its area forming hanging gardens, paved areas, statues, fountains and water gardens.

Early Roman gardens were modelled on Greek designs, with courtyards filled with pots, tubs, troughs and window boxes. A citizen's wealth could be measured by the size of his garden. After the fire in AD 64, Nero had many houses demolished to allow the construction of a large and elaborate garden.

In the heyday of the Roman Empire, the rose was a symbol of mystery and secrecy, and roses were thought to cure dissolute behaviour caused by an excess of wine. Guests at banquets were showered with rose petals to ameliorate drunkenness, and the flowers were imported when they were out of season. Later the Romans developed ingenious techniques for growing roses with 'hot beds' warmed by hot water.

Roman town gardens were usually small and walled. Often the walls were painted with garden scenes to make them appear larger. Wealthy Romans had villas outside the city, with sumptuous gardens incorporating views of the surrounding countryside. Flowers played a minor role; gardens were planted with shrubs and decorated with statues and urns.

Islamic gardens

From about the seventh century AD, Arab armies carried the Islamic faith both east and west. When these invaders first saw the Persian gardens, they were

convinced they embodied the Paradise promised in the Koran to the faithful. Incidentally, the English word 'paradise' is derived from *pairidaeza,* an Old Persian word meaning 'enclosure'.

The Arabs spread westward, through North Africa to Andalusia, in Spain, where, at Cordoba in the eighth century, they began a garden which was modelled on one in Damascus.

This invasion of people and the introduction of new ideas also resulted in a great influx of plants into Europe, including many 'exotics' previously only known in Persia and the East. But perhaps the most enduring legacy of Islamic gardens has been courtyard gardens and their use of water. The cloister-like and contemplative ambience of Moorish gardens has a positive, healing quality that soothes the spirit and gives reassurance of life's continuity.

The Islamic concept of designing buildings to form an inner courtyard protected from the outside world was adopted throughout much of Spain. The design created a peaceful haven away from the noise and the stress of the city as well as providing continuous, rotational shade. When the Spaniards settled in the south-western parts of North America, they continued building courtyard gardens, a style particularly suited to the hot, dry climate in that part of the continent. The design of these dwellings, where an inner courtyard is open to the sky, took its name from the word Spanish *patio,* which literally means

'courtyard'. The meaning has been stretched in English usage to mean any paved area. Sadly, larger paved areas, known as terraces, are now almost invariably called 'patios'. Terraces were revered in Renaissance Europe, and were decorated with pots and statues. They were often elevated to provide a view.

Early monastery gardens

Gardening played an important part in the first Christian monastery, founded by St Anthony in Egypt in AD 305. A few years later, St Jerome's advice to a young man about to begin monastic life was: 'Hoe your ground, set out cabbages and convey water to the conduits.'

In the early sixth century, St Benedict became a monk at Subiaco, Italy, and is said to have planted a rose garden; he later founded the famous monastery at Monte Cassino, south of Rome.

During the early part of the ninth century, Walafrid Strabo (AD 809–849) was Abbot at Reichenau Abbey on an island in Lake Constance (which borders Switzerland, Germany and Austria, and has the Rhine flowing through it). He wrote of plants in his garden and the nature of gardening:

> Though a life of retreat offers various joys,
> None, I think, will compare with the time one employs
> In the study of herbs, or in striving to gain
> Some practical knowledge of nature's domain.
> Get a garden! What kind you may get matters not.

Records suggest he personally grew twenty-three plants, and he mentioned a dozen or so others.

During the beginning of the ninth century, plans for the ideal monastery garden were originated at the monastery of St Gall, Switzerland. The plans included a wide range of plants such as cumin, fennel, fenugreek, purple iris, lovage, mint, pennyroyal, roses, rosemary, rue and sage. In all, about forty-nine plants were mentioned.

Slightly earlier, Charlemagne the Great (AD 742–814) issued a decree listing about eighty-nine plants to grow on Crown estates throughout his empire.

Ha-Ha

Few garden features capture as much interest and amusement as a ha-ha (also known as haw-haw or sunk fence), It is a ditch that creates a barrier to people and animals, yet allows uninterrupted views over the boundary. It is said to have been used by French landscape designers in the seventeenth century, and to have gained its name from people who, when suddenly coming across it, said, 'Ah! Ah!' It was popularized in Britain by the famous landscape gardener Lancelot 'Capability' Brown (1716–1783).

TEA GARDENS

The tea garden played an important role in the preparatory ritual to a tea ceremony; it was where those taking part would assemble and cast off worldly cares before drinking tea. The purpose of the garden was to encourage a feeling of serenity and to direct thoughts, not to confuse and distract them; trees, shrubs and ferns created a timeless and contemplative landscape, not confused with flowers that, by their ephemeral nature and colour, are a continuing reminder of the changing seasons of nature.

His list included medicinal herbs, fruit trees, carrots and parsnips. In addition, madder (an important cloth dye) and teasel (which has stiff, hooked bracts used to raise the pile on cloth) were mentioned.

Chinese and Japanese gardens

China has a long tradition of garden design. Two separate philosophies have influenced them: Daoism (or Taoism) seeks to discover and portray how Man can best fit into the world, while Confucianism concentrates on Man's relationship with other people and with himself.

In Chinese gardens, the house and garden are invariably conceived as separate entities, with the garden reflecting the Daoist philosophy, and the house, with its courtyards and rooms, portraying the Confucian element. The garden may also have buildings to enhance meditation and contemplation.

The design of Japanese gardens is said to have been influenced in the seventh century by a visit from a Japanese ambassador to China. Early Japanese gardens were also influenced by Shintoism, a religion that sees Man, animals, plants and all natural things as equals and to be respected both individually and collectively. Gardens with these ideals encouraged the creation of natural scenes, meticulously formed and maintained, to reflect the beauty of nature. They also create an atmosphere of peace, contemplation and tranquillity.

BODHIDHARMA, THE CHINESE PATRON OF THE TEA PLANT

Bodhidharma, an Indian credited with establishing Zen Buddhism. According to legend he cut off his eyelids in anger after falling asleep in meditation. The first tea plant grew where they fell, which is why Zen Buddhists drink tea to stay awake during meditation.

Facing page: Many religions, including Christianity, envisage paradise as a garden. This painting from 1410 shows a 'paradise garden'.

Left: Daitakuji Temple, Kyoto, Japan, reveals the tranquillity and peace created by Japanese gardens.

DOES SOIL HAVE A SOUL?

*All life depends on soil, and many cultures and religions have considered Earth
to have a soul, a sensitivity and innermost living force. For that reason
it was believed that land could not be owned and that humans were
merely its caretakers, preserving it for future generations.*

Nomadic peoples never considered that land could be owned. They roamed the earth with their animals, adding fertility to the soil and reaping its harvests before passing on to other land. Human life was lived according to the rhythm of the seasons, just as it was for many birds and other animals. For millions of years man lived and harvested the land in this way.

SETTLED COMMUNITIES

With the onset of settled communities, there gradually arose an understanding that Man was a shaper of the environment and did not have to adhere to its dictates. While he could not change the seasons, he could organize his husbandry and feed himself without having to roam before the winds of chance.

As land was cultivated, there arose a folklore that reminded people of the yearly cycle of country life, of the times to plough, sow crops and harvest them. Nowadays, these rhymes are all too frequently thought to be archaic and to have no bearing on modern life, but it is clear that they present a tapestry of country life, when many country folk could not read and had only their observations and experience to guide them. These rhymes arose throughout the world. In North America, early settlers were advised by Native Americans that only when the whiteoak, elm and hickory leaves in the hills, and osage orange leaves on the plains, were the size of a squirrel's ears was it safe to plant corn. This saying made clear the plant's nature, which is frost-tender, and must not be sown until after all risk of frost has passed.

In England a variation was:

When the elm leaf is as big as a mouse's ear,
Then time to sow barley, never fear.

The progress of other plants was not the only guideline offered by these old rhymes; others refer to the church calendar:

When the parson begins to read Genesis,
it's time to sow black oats.

OF LIFE ITSELF

Soil is the stuff of life: a complex mass of minerals, dead and decomposing organic material, macroscopic organisms, water and air. When all of these are in balance, plants thrive, but lack of one or more creates impoverished soil and detrimentally influences the germination of seeds and growth of plants.

Facing page: Bluebells are the epitome of late spring, when flowers and fresh shoots herald the onset of summer.

Above centre: Each year the germination of seeds and emergence of seedlings above the soil's surface have a mystical quality that appears to restate the reliance of life itself on soil.

Above: Soils vary enormously. Some are full of flint and chalk, making them well drained and alkaline (a); ethers ore loam-like and fertile (b); some are mainly formed of clay that makes them heavy to cultivate (c); Improving soil is possible, although it usually takes several seasons. Manure and garden compost improve both sandy and clay soils; chopped bark (d) is ideal as a mulch for intermixing with soil. Ground limestone (e) decreases acidity, as well as improving soils heavy in clay. Sharp sand (f) breaks up clay soil, improving its drainage.

Below: Soil-testing kits enable the acidity or alkalinity of soil to be determined.

TYPES OF SOIL

Gardeners generally seek a loam with a fertile and moisture-retentive nature, containing neither too much clay nor excessive amounts of sand. But nature is not usually that obliging, and many gardens have light, sandy soil that drains quickly, leaching its nutrients, or heavy clay that is either cold and waterlogged or baked dry. However, it is always possible to make improvements, either through cultivation techniques or by adding soil-improving materials.

ASSESSING SOIL

Knowing a soil's make-up is the first step in its improvement. To quickly see if it is predominantly clay or sand, fill a tall screw-top jar a quarter full with soil and then add water until three-quarters full. Shake vigorously and allow the mixture to settle into layers of different materials. Stones immediately fall to the bottom, then coarse and light sand, silt and the very fine particles of clay. Organic material floats on the surface. The proportions of these materials indicate a soil's nature.

Also, picking up a handful of soil and rubbing it between a forefinger and thumb is another test. If it creates a slippery, smooth, greasy surface, it contains a high proportion of clay, but if it feels rough and gritty, it is predominantly sandy.

An additional way is to slightly moisten some soil, roll it into a thin rod and curl it to form a ring. The smaller the diameter of the ring it can form without breaking, the higher its clay content.

Alkaline or acid? The acidity or alkalinity of soil are measured on a pH scale, which ranges from 0 to 14, with 7.0 as neutral. Soils below pH 7.0 are increasingly acid, whereas above that figure they are increasingly alkaline. However, most plants grow best in a slightly acid soil, about pH 6.5.

Soil-testing kits assess the pH: mix some soil with water and add the testing chemical, and compare the resulting colour against a chart. An alternative – and especially useful for those who are red-green colour blind – is a pH meter.

IMPROVING YOUR SOIL

All soils can be improved, although it can be a long and continuous process.

Clay soils These are heavy and sticky to dig in winter, and often waterlogged, while in summer they often become baked and cracked. Installing land drains will remove surplus water, but it is essential for growing most plants to lighten the soil by incorporating large amounts of organic materials. In a vegetable garden, double digging in the winter helps by increasing the aeration.

Sandy soils These are light, easy to cultivate and quick to warm up in spring, enabling early seed sowing.

Unfortunately, nutrients rapidly leach from sandy soils, and manure or garden compost needs to be added each year. Also, mulch the surface of the soil in hot, dry weather, to maintain moisture, and water regularly.

Acid soils Dust the surface with either hydrated lime or ground limestone in winter. The amount needed depends on the pH, the soil type, and whether ground limestone or hydrated lime is used. The following amounts decrease acidity by I.0 pH:

Soil	Hydrated Lime	Ground Limestone
CLAY	600g/sq m	800g/sq m
LOAM	420g/sq m	540g/sq m
SAND	210g/sq m	270g/sq m

Alkaline soils Dig in plenty of manure or garden compost, and use acidic fertilizers such as sulphate of ammonia.

PREPARING THE SOIL

However inhospitable some parts of the world may initially appear, they usually support some kind of vegetation; even the freezing tundra of Alaska and Siberia, swamp-like everglades of Florida, windswept land of Tierra Del Fuego, or saline-steeped shores throughout the world have an abundance of plants. It would therefore be easy and logical for gardeners always to grow local plants; but such is the perverseness and enthusiasm of gardeners that invariably their greatest desire is to

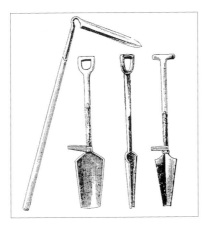

grow plants native to the other side of the world! Plants from alpine regions can be seen growing in flat, temperate areas hundreds of miles from any mountain range, while roses, which are native mainly to temperate regions in the northern hemisphere, are

enthusiastically grown in tropical and arid areas of Australia. However, success in growing the majority of plants in all places depends on the health and fertility of the soil.

Draining the land

Making sure excess water drains freely through the soil is essential; unless air reaches the roots of plants they die, and waterlogged soil soon kills many beneficial organisms. Waterlogging usually occurs in soils predominantly formed of clay, in which individual particles are very small. Conversely, sandy soil allows rapid drainage, but during summer becomes depleted of water, and the problem is to encourage the retention of moisture.

MYTHS AND LEGENDS

Goddesses played an important role in early cultures and religions. The fifteenth-century Aztec earth goddess Coaticue is said to bring fertility to the soil.

Top centre: These drainage tools were used in the late 1800s to form trenches in which drainage tiles were laid.

Left: Azaleas create a feast of colour in spring and early summer and are ideal for planting in acid soil.

BEAUTIFYING THE FACE

As well as pigments derived from plants and animals, earth was used by Native Americans to adorn their faces and other ports of their bodies. Early Egyptians (above) employed coloured soils and clays to beautify their bodies, while Roman men and women used cosmetics. Nero used ceruse (white lead) and chalk to whiten his face.

If your garden becomes awash with water in winter and remains so for several weeks, then the installation of drains is essential. Another indication of the necessity for drains is the presence of rushes and sedges. If you are uncertain, dig a test hole.

In winter, dig a deep hole and monitor the water level until early spring. If it remains level with the surface for long periods, then drains are essential. Cover the hole to prevent accidents. Or you could simply see this as a marvellous opportunity to plant a bog garden.

Ways to drain soil

The simplest drain is a ditch dug around the plot; although this is possible on an agricultural scale – and forms the basis of early attempts to drain land – it is not practical in a garden. A variation of this method was to dig trenches (also known as open drains) across the land, and to feed the water into a ditch. A later method was to partially fill each trench with compacted brushwood (mostly ash), and to add soil until level with the surrounding land. Brushwood drains worked best in stiff, clay soils. A later variation of this type of drain was to fill trenches to about half their depth with rubble; round stones were preferred to those with sharp edges. Pieces of turf were laid upside-down on top of the rubble to prevent topsoil filtering through to the base and clogging the drain. Nowadays, a single or double layer of thick plastic sheeting is used to separate soil from stones.

On a large scale, although rubble drains appeared cheap to construct, it was difficult in some areas to get stones. Also, in winter, when drains were usually constructed, it was impossible to trans port the stones in carts across wet fields and along country roads.

Tiles shaped like horseshoes were used, but were expensive and relatively scarce. Then, in about 1845, clay pipe drains were made commercially and in large numbers, and for many years served as the main way to drain soil.

Pipe drains Up to the latter part of the twentieth century, clay, unglazed pipes about 30 cm long and 3 cm wide were used as main drains, with 10 cm wide types as side or feeder drains. These were laid in trenches with a slight slope to a ditch or sump. Nowadays, perforated, ribbed flexible drainpipes, 8 cm in diameter and in rolls about 25 m long, are readily available and are far easier and quicker to lay. Dig trenches 60–75 cm deep and 30–45 cm wide, with a minimum slope of 1 in 90 towards an outlet. Spread a 5cm thick layer of rock along the trench's base, and place the plastic tubing on top. Where a side drain joins the main one, cut it at an angle so that the two pipes butt together closely. Place a double layer of thick plastic over the joint and for about 45 cm around it. Spread a 8–10 cm thick layer of rock over the pipes, then cover the drain with the topsoil.

Ditch or sump? Few gardeners have a stream or ditch bordering their garden into which excess water can be drained. If you do, allow the end of the pipe to extend about 8 cm into the ditch, and ensure the outfall is above the expected height of the water after torrential winter storms. Also, push a piece of crumpled wire or plastic netting into the pipe to prevent vermin gaining entry.

MEDICINAL AND COSMETIC USES OF MUD

Earth has played an important medicinal and cosmetic role in our lives. Mud baths, which are usually prepared from muddy deposits found near hot springs, act as a large poultice when applied to the surface of the body. This increases the body's temperature and accelerates the pulse rate by six to twelve beats a minute. Respiration increases and the recipient perspires profusely.

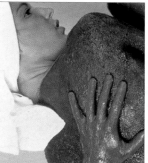

Mud baths have been used to treat gout and rheumatism. Mud packs are well known in beauty treatments for women. Traditionally, they were made from an absorbent clay (known as fuller's earth), glycerine and benzoin. However, spa towns often have their own mixtures, and many are reputed to have medicinal qualities. In ancient Rome, crocodile dung was used as a face pack!

To construct a sump, dig a hole about 1.2 m square, and deep enough so that its base is at least 30 cm lower than the bottom of the pipe that drains into it. Fill the sump to half its depth with large stones or clean, broken bricks, then to within 30 cm of the surface with gravel. Cover this with a double layer of strong plastic or inverted turves, and top up with topsoil.

SOIL CULTIVATION

Because the first step in cultivating soil is to remove trees and scrub, the sowing of seeds probably began along the Nile river or in the Tigris–Euphrates valley. There, the soil is deep and fertile, yet because of the low rainfall it is relatively free of tall, woody vegetation. Also, the weather was warm and uniform, and the

yearly floodwater – which both raised the water level in the soil and provided irrigation for crops as the land began to dry – meant that the crude soil-tilling implements of early Man could be used with relative ease.

Cultivating the soil, in the forms of digging, ploughing or forking, opens it up and encourages the penetration of air and water. Early Egyptians developed a wooden plough drawn by oxen yoked together; wooden spades soon wear and break, especially in stony soils, but it was not until the eighteenth century that modern developments in ploughs began, with James Small in Scotland and Thomas Jefferson in North America. However, it is worth remembering that medieval spades were made of wood but had the blade sheathed in metal to make it more durable.

Of course, hand-powered tools were in use from earliest times, and some early ploughs were pushed by foot through the soil or given greater penetration by using the chest.

Digging soil Digging is fundamental to keeping soil healthy and preparing for planting and sowing. Apart from increasing the aeration and drainage in soil, digging in autumn and exposing the surface to frost, wind and rain during winter creates a fine tilth into which seeds can be sown in spring. Digging also buries and kills annual weeds and exposes the larvae of soil pests, such as cockchafer grubs, to frost and birds.

Single- and double-digging are the two main soil cultivation techniques, although there are others. For instance, ridging involves digging the ground into ridges 50 cm apart and 20–25 cm high, formed down a slope to increase drainage. By exposing a larger than normal area of soil to winter frosts, ridging produces more friable soil by spring. In bastard trenching, the soil is dug to twice the depth of a spade's blade, and the soil at the level of a third spade's depth is broken up with a garden fork.

Single-digging This is by far the most usual method of digging, and involves systematically inverting the soil to the depth of a spade's blade. While doing this, annual weeds can be buried and well-rotted manure or garden compost can be mixed with the soil.

Above: Medieval spades were made of tough wood, with the cutting edges covered in metal to make them more durable.

Left: The noble Sennufer sniffs appreciatively at a lotus flower while his wife sits beside him. The lotus is one of the two symbols of Upper Egypt; the other is the papyrus.

Below: Bog gardens are ideal where land is naturally moist; plant these areas with moisture-loving plants such as border primulas and *Iris ensata* (earlier known as *I. kaempferi*) and *I. laevigata*.

Mark off a strip of soil 30 cm wide at one end of the plot, dig a trench 25–30 cm deep (the depth of a spade's blade) across the complete plot, and transport the soil to the other end of the plot. Then, dig systematically along the trench by inverting blocks of soil – each 8–10 cm thick, 18 cm wide and to the depth of a spade's blade – so that they fall upside-down against the far side of the trench. If the soil is densely covered with grass or annual weeds, before starting to dig each row skim them off and place them upside-down in the trench's base. Remove and burn all perennial weeds, such a docks, thistles, horsetail, bindweed and couch grass. Keep the overall surface of the land level. When digging is complete, the soil from the first trench – previously moved to the other end of the plot – can be placed in the last one.

Double-digging This method of digging is usually restricted to where land has been neglected for many years or where pasture land is being turned into a garden. It is also an ideal technique where the drainage is poor.

The first task is to mark a strip of land (using a garden line or just scratching an indentation on the soil's surface) 60 cm wide at one end of the plot and digging a 25–30 cm deep trench. Barrow the soil to the other end of the plot.

Use a garden fork to dig over the soil in the trench's base; also, skim off grass and annual weeds from the next 60 cm wide strip of soil, and place them in the trench. At the same time, add well-decayed manure or garden compost. Then dig the soil from the next 60 cm wide strip into the first one, so that another trench is formed from where the soil was taken. Now repeat the process until the complete plot is dug and the soil from the first trench can be placed in the last one.

MANURES AND FERTILIZERS

Creating and maintaining soil fertility, so that plants can be grown on the same piece of land year after year, was a desire of early farmers, and is an essential part of gardening today. A characteristic of slash-and-burn agriculture was the cultivation of land until it was exhausted of nutrients. Then, fresh land was cleared, cropped and, later, abandoned. However, where rivers spread silt over surrounding fields every year, this maintained fertility.

Techniques for keeping soil fertile and 'in good heart' were known to the Romans, who understood the value of

VENETIAN GARDENING TOOLS

This image of garden tools appeared in Giardino di Agricultura, *published in Venice in 1593. Many of the tools are easily recognizable today, and include spades, draw hoes, sickles, bill-hooks, saws and rakes.*

Right: Single digging, to the depth of a spade's blade, is the usual method of preparing soil in winter. Make a strip of soil 30cm wide across one end of the plot (*top left*). Use a spade to remove the turf (*top right*). Dig a trench to the depth of the spade's blade and place this at the other end of the plot (*bottom left*). Systematically dig along the edge of the trench, turning blocks of soil upside down (*bottom right*). When digging is complete, put soil from the first trench into the last one.

animal manure. This was practical and continued in parts of Europe where animals were fenced in, but during the expansion of farming in North America, animals were more likely to be allowed to roam freely, so manure could not be collected. And in any case, the apparently limitless supply of virgin land with its often remarkable fertility did not encourage great interest in soil husbandry. When the land did eventually become barren through repeated cropping, it was sometimes necessary to leave it fallow for fifteen years or more. Much later, farmers in New England relied on fish and rockweed (a coarse, brown seaweed which grows attached to rocks), while in southern states marl and cowpeas (a sprawling, pea-like plant) were added to the soil. Swamp and creek mud was also used to improve sandy soil. About the middle of the 1800s, farmers in North America started to put great reliance on fertilizers and tried Peruvian guano, Chilean nitrates and Carolina phosphates to produce larger crops.

SOIL IMPROVERS

These are 'bulky' materials which, when added to soil, help to improve aeration and drainage, as well as encouraging the presence of soil organisms that make the chemicals in fertilizers available to plants.

Manure

Also known as horse or chicken manure, this is a traditional soil improver, as well as

supplying plant foods such as nitrogen. It also provides trace elements, required in tiny amounts, but vital to plants. Manure is best dug into the soil during winter digging, or added as a surface mulch. It must be matured for several weeks or it will burn plants. Both clay and sandy soils benefit from yearly applications of it.

Peat

For many years this was dug into soil, especially to improve the water-retention

of light, sandy soil. However, its removal from peat beds destroys the natural habitats of many animals, birds and insects, so alternatives should be sought.

Garden compost

Formed from the decomposition of plants and vegetable waste from kitchens, this is ideal for adding to soil. However, although it can be made in free-standing heaps, it is better to use special compost bins.

Left: The Spring, by Flemish artist Jacob Grimmer (*circa* 1629–1689), shows gardeners raking, sowing, digging, planting and pruning.

Mushroom compost

Its availability depends on mushrooms being grown locally. It is bulky and helps in soil aeration and, especially, the retention of moisture, but it is alkaline and therefore best reserved for use in acid soils.

Spent hops

This is the residue of hops after the brewing of beer, and is ideal for adding to light, sandy soil to encourage the retention of moisture.

Seaweed

In many coastal areas seaweed is an important manure; it is usually collected after heavy storms have deposited it on beaches (but first check if it is legal to gather it). It is ideal for digging into soil, and although it contains less nitrogen and phosphate than manure, it is richer in potassium. When used to increase the moisture content in sandy soil, for which

Below: Frogs, as well as toads, slow-worms, and hedgehogs, eat significant amounts of slugs and can be encouraged into gardens by the construction of a pond.

it is ideal, it must be dug in before it becomes too dry.

Sand

Although expensive when used to improve large areas, coarse sharp sand helps with the drainage of heavy, clay soil.

RAISED BEDS AND TERRACING

Where soil is excessively wet and difficult to drain, raised beds help to create areas where plants can be safely grown. Dig out the subsoil, fill the base with clean rubble, construct side constraints (with natural stone, bricks, planks of wood or stout logs) and fill the bed with friable topsoil. Leave it to settle, then put in the plants.

Raised beds are also useful where the soil is excessively alkaline or acid, allowing a wider range of plants to be grown.

ROTATING GARDEN CROPS

In vegetable plots it is essential to rotate crops to make sure the soil is not continually depleted of the same plant foods; rotation also prevents the build-up of pests and diseases specific to certain plants. In addition, rotating crops means that over a period of a few years the complete plot receives a variety of treatments. For example, when growing potatoes the soil is repeatedly earthed-up around shoots, which both prevents the growth of weeds and encourages the creation of friable soil.

Vegetables vary in the amounts of lime and manure they require. For example, to

CATCH CROPPING

A technique also known as 'inter-cropping', catch cropping enables fast-growing, fast- maturing crops such as radishes and lettuces to be grown between rows of slow-growing plants like leeks and trench celery.

grow potatoes neither lime nor manure are needed, whereas the brassica family (cabbages, cauliflowers and Brussels sprouts, for example) requires manure, as well as lime if the soil is acid. However, pulses (peas and beans), lettuces, aubergines, onions, squash and corn need generous applications of garden compost or well-decayed manure.

There are several ways to create a successful rotation of vegetable plots to produce the best crops, some with a cycle of three years, others for four. The following scheme is for three years.

Planning the rotation of crops

Divide a vegetable plot into three equal parts; each should then contain one of three groups of different vegetables, which will be rotated in the sequence indicated below.

Group One includes root vegetables, such as beetroots, carrots, endive, parsnips, salsify, Jerusalem artichokes and scorzonera. Potatoes are usually included in this group. When preparing the soil, dig in winter, but add neither lime nor manure. Instead, rake in a general-purpose fertilizer a couple of weeks before planting or sowing.

Group Two includes Brussels sprouts, cabbages, cauliflowers, kale, kohlrabi, radishes, swedes and turnips. When preparing the soil, dig during winter and mix in a good garden compost or a well-decayed manure. If the soil is acid, dress the surface with lime, but not at the same time as adding manure. About two weeks before sowing seeds or setting young plants in position, rake a good general-purpose fertilizer into the surface soil.

Group Three includes aubergine, beans, green peppers, celery, cucumbers, chicory, leeks, lettuce, squash, onions, peas, spinach, corn and tomatoes. When preparing the soil, dig it in winter and mix in garden compost or well-decayed manure. If the soil is acid, dust it with lime, but not at the same time as adding manure. About two weeks before sowing seeds or putting in tender young plants, rake a general-purpose fertilizer into the soil to give your plants the best start possible.

CONSERVING MOISTURE IN THE SOIL

Reducing the rate at which moisture evaporates from the soil's surface has long been a problem, especially in sunny regions with low rainfall. The Romans knew the value of mulching with stones; both Virgil in the first century BC and Lucius Columella in the first century AD recommended this method of moisture conservation, especially around grapes

Left: Raised beds ensure the soil does not become waterlogged and cold. Mix plenty of decomposed organic material such as garden compost into the soil to ensure fertility and to help retain moisture.

SHADUF

This early method of irrigation was used by the Egyptians to raise water from the Nile so that crops could be watered. It consists of a pivoted pole with a counterbalance that enables a bucket to be lowered and raised with ease.

Facing page: Cabbages with dark and attractive leaves can be grown among ornamental plants to create variations in colour, shape and size.

Right Spreading a mulch between plants helps to reduce weed growth, conserves moisture in the ground and adds to fertility. First, however, dig up perennial weeds and hoe off annual types.

and apricots. They knew that it kept land cool in summer and protected light soil during heavy rain. However, the Romans do not appear to have used organic mulches.

In addition to covering the surface, using a hoe to disturb surface soil helps to reduce moisture loss. Hoeing off or pulling up weeds also helps reduce the loss of moisture.

The advantages of mulches

The many advantages of mulching include the obvious one of conserving moisture in soil, but there are others. During summer, mulches keep the soil cool, preventing roots being damaged by excessively high temperatures. Conversely, in winter they protect roots from low temperatures, especially ground

frost. When soil is not mulched, torrential rain splashes plants with mud; this is a particular problem with strawberries.

When mulches of garden compost and well-decayed manure are used, this adds fertility to the soil. There are two main types of mulching materials – organic and non-organic.

Organic mulches: These are derived from plants and animals, and as well as creating mulches, they eventually decay and provide nutrients for plants.

Before creating a mulch – usually in spring or early summer – remove all weeds (dig up and burn perennial types such as docks and thistles) and water the soil thoroughly to a depth of at least 10 cm; even if weeds are not present, disturb the soil's surface thoroughly and evenly

to make sure that water can penetrate rather than running off a hard, impenetrable surface.

Form a 5–8 cm thick mulch around plants, but not in contact with them. During summer, organic mulches decay, and by autumn little of them may remain. In late autumn or early winter, lightly fork the mulch into the soil, taking care not to damage the roots of trees, shrubs and herbaceous perennials.

Manure: This is ideal, because it provides more nutrition for plants than any other mulch. During dry periods, however, it may be blown about.

Garden compost: This is created from vegetable kitchen waste and soft-tissued plants from gardens. After decomposition it forms a material that is ideal for placing around plants.

Peat: In earlier times this was frequently recommended as a mulch, but its removal from peat beds destroys the natural environments of many animals, birds and insects. Also, when used as a mulch it often becomes dry and is blown about by the wind or disturbed by birds.

Bark chippings: These create an effective and attractive mulch, especially in ornamental gardens and around shrubs and trees. Unfortunately, during dry periods bark chipping tends to be disturbed by birds.

Wood chippings: These are created by shredding machines – which can be hired – into which woody stems and twigs are fed to be chopped up. Birds often scatter the chippings in summer, but

nevertheless this can be an inexpensive way to produce mulching material.

Grass cuttings: This is an inexpensive mulching material, but do not use it if the lawn has been recently treated with weedkillers. Form a mulch only 2.5 cm thick, and keep it away from the stems of plants. Also, because grass cuttings retain moisture and become warm as they decompose, they often attract snails and slugs.

Straw: This is often used as a mulch in strawberry beds, where it also prevents heavy rainstorms damaging the fruit. A layer of straw makes access possible even when the soil between plants is muddy, but it can be a fire hazard, and when dry it may be blown about or disturbed by birds. At the end of summer it does not readily decay, and its breakdown depletes the soil of nitrogen.

Sawdust: At one time this was popular in areas where sawmills made it readily available. Unfortunately, it often becomes compacted during wet seasons, while in dry weather it blows about. In North America it was widely used to mulch blackberries.

Newspapers: Sometimes these are classified among non-organic mulching materials, but as they are mainly derived from wood pulp, they are classified as organic here. However, when laid around plants they do not look attractive, and therefore are best restricted to vegetable plots.

Sod mulching: The terminology is North American, but the philosophy is

common to many countries, where it is known as 'grassing down'. Encouraging grass to grow between apple trees in orchards helps to decrease vegetative growth and to encourage trees to develop fruits at an early stage; the fruits are also more highly coloured. In North America, alfalfa and Ladino clover, as well as ordinary grasses, have been used to create the sward. The practice in North America was to form a sward between the trees, then to lay a mulch of hay, straw, strawy manure or sawdust close to the trees, but not touching them.

Other materials: The hulls of buckwheat and cottonseed have been used to mulch roses in North America, while in southern states pine needles were used to mulch strawberry plants. In addition, ground corn cobs and tobacco stems have been used to mulch roses, lilies, irises and peonies in North America.

MAN EATING SOIL

Geophagy, or earth-eating, has long been practised by Man – as a medicine, to gain extra vitamins, or as part of a sacramental ritual.

Soil was employed by Native Americans when preparing acorn meal; one part clay to about twenty of ground acorns was used. The clay was said to make the mixture rise when cooked and to give the bread a distinctive sweetness.

In the late 1800s it was reported that earlier, in the Scottish Highlands, cakes of iron-manganese were eaten after large meals. In New Guinea, soapstone (also known as steatite, a white-to-green talc with a soapy feel) was preferred. Dyaks of Borneo were said to eat a mixture of red ochre and an oily clay, while the Hopi Indians in North America ate clay mixed with potatoes.

Non-organic mulches: These consist mainly of black plastic and a few household materials.

Black plastic: This is increasingly used to conserve moisture and to suppress the growth of weeds. When placed on soil early in the year, it helps the ground to warm up, thereby enabling seeds to be sown earlier than normal and young plants to be planted.

Old carpets: These are mainly used in vegetable plots, but take care that they do not create homes for slugs, snails, earwigs and millepedes, especially in warm, wet weather.

ORGANIC GARDENING

Growing garden plants without the use of artificial fertilizers and sprays has become an increasingly important part of gardening. It is also a growing concern in the commercial production of food. Living with our global neighbours, both near and far, and raising food uncontaminated by toxic chemicals has become the endeavour of many people.

In 1940, Sir Albert Howard published ideas about natural farming, advocating the use of natural manures and abhorring chemical fertilizers. Twenty years later, in

Right: Cabbage root flies can quickly devastate cabbages and other brassica plants. To prevent this, place a collar of carpet or underlay around each stem.

the early 1960s Rachel Carson, American naturalist and aquatic biologist, wrote *Silent Spring*, which attacked the indiscriminate use of pesticides. She highlighted the way pesticides were entering and poisoning the animal, bird and human food chains. At the end of the foreword Lord Shackleton wrote for Miss Carson's book, he suggested:

> Miners use canaries to warn them of deadly gases. It might not be a bad idea if we took the same warning from the dead birds in our countryside.

In many countries there followed a realization of an impending catastrophe from the use of chemicals, initiating research into growing plants in a way harmonious with nature.

Growing plants naturally

The nutrition provided by organic fertilizers and manures has to be 'unlocked' by a vast army of soil organisms, including worms, minute bacteria and fungi. Because the releasing of plant foods is a relatively slow process, most organic fertilizers and manures have a long-lasting and consistent effect. An additional benefit of organic gardening is that it encourages the presence of essential soil organisms, making the entire process self-perpetuating and more efficient as time passes.

The advantages of organic over non-organic gardening are:

Soil fertility is maintained without 'poisoning' the soil. By adding manure,

the structure of the soil is improved, enabling air to enter and moisture to be retained. In addition, the damaging effect of torrential rain on a soil's surface is minimized.

Weeds can be controlled by mulching rather than by the use of weedkillers, which may cause damage to wildlife and pondlife.

The natural control and prevention of pests and diseases can be practised by digging soil in winter – the larvae of soil pests become exposed to birds and cold weather. Rotating crops helps prevent the build-up of pests and diseases.

Encouraging wildlife into gardens assists in controlling pests. Wildlife ponds are invaluable and encourage the presence of hedgehogs, frogs and toads, which feed on slugs.

By choosing disease-resistant varieties of vegetables, there is a reduction in the incidence of diseases.

Companion planting helps to deter some pests – garlic, leeks and onions mask the scent of carrots which attracts carrot flies; planting chives between roses reduces the incidence of greenfly.

Where pests are present, use safer, organic pesticides such as pyrethrum, derris and nicotine, which are non-persistent in the soil and non-systemic (they do not enter a plant's tissue and make it poisonous). There are also organic fungicides, such as Bordeaux mixture (a mixture of copper sulphate, hydrated lime and water), a preparation used to control potato blight.

Natural predators

Nature plays a large and important role in controlling garden pests by providing natural predators. These attack and eat plant pests, and dramatically reduce damage to plants. Beneficial insects must be treated with care and encouraged into gardens. Chemical sprays soon kill them, but organic mulches attract ground beetles and rove beetles; groups of yellow flowers attract hoverflies. Carrots, parsnips, and fennel encourage the presence of parasitic wasps and lacewings. Here is a range of beneficial insects:

Braconid flies lay eggs in caterpillars, especially those of the highly damaging cabbage white butterfly. Also, a few attack greenfly. The eggs hatch and the young grubs live inside their hosts, eventually killing them.

Chalcid wasps attack butterflies, moths, flies and scale insects. There are several types: *Encarsa formosa* is especially effective at controlling greenhouse whitefly, while in orchards others attack woolly aphids.

Above: Some parasitic wasps lay their eggs so that when the young hatch they have a ready supply of aphids and other garden pests.

Braconid fly

Chalcid wasp

VIOLET GROUND BEETLES

These agile beetles, with violet edges to their wing-cases, can frequently be seen climbing among surface soil. They do not like strong sunlight and usually hunt at night, especially under damp conditions.

Below: Snails, as well as slugs, are voracious eaters of tender plants and, if unchecked, quickly destroy large areas of plants. Use proprietary baits as well as beer and sugar traps to kill them.

Green lacewings have a delicate appearance, but both adults and larvae are voracious eaters of aphids and other soft-bodied garden pests.

Ground beetles, such as the Violet Ground Beetle, are agile and have strong jaws. They live in the soil and eat soft-tissued grubs and the adults of pests, including slugs and cabbage rootfly eggs.

Hoverflies 'hover' in midair. Some of them are pests, but many have larvae that feed on greenfly.

Ichneumon flies lay eggs in caterpillars. They hatch and eat their host, leaving just the skin. Some ichneumon flies attack the larvae of apple blossom weevils.

Ladybugs, both as grubs and adults, eat greenfly, scale insects, mealy bugs and thrips. There are many types of ladybug, and an adult often eats as many as 15 to 20 aphids a day.

Rove beetles, such as the Devil's Coach-horse, have narrow bodies and live in soil. Both adults and larvae eat mites and the pupae of cabbage rootflies.

ANIMALS EATING SOIL

Many animals eat soil to alleviate ailments or to add chemicals to their diets. Chimpanzees suffering stomach upsets know the benefit of eating soil: they break pieces of soil off termite mounds and eat them. This soil contains large amounts of clay minerals which are a form of kaolin. Indeed, kaolin has long been used to treat intestinal problems such as diarrhoea in humans; sometimes the kaolin is mixed with morphine.

Elephants in rainforests, where soils and plants are deficient in minerals such as sodium, may lick rocks that have a high salt content. In the Mount Elgon region, along the Kenya-Uganda border, elephants sometimes enter caves in search of rocks that are rich in salts. In addition, an elephant will use its tusks to disturb and scoop out mineral-rich soil.

Orang-utans eat mineral-rich soil, while gorillas will instinctively search for minerals in the soil when their bodies are low in them. Mountain gorillas have been known to chew volcanic soil that is rich in sodium and potassium.

Cultural pest control measures

Several cultural techniques help prevent insects attacking plants:

Blackfly damage on broad beans is reduced by pinching out the tips of autumn-sown beans in summer, as soon as four trusses of pods have formed.

Cabbage root flies chew the roots of cabbages and other brassica plants. Deter them by hanging strips of kerosene-impregnated blanket or sacking from canes to prevent the flies scenting young plants and laying eggs on them. An alternative way to prevent the flies laying eggs at the bases of stems as to cut 13 cm square pieces of carpet. Cut a slit to the center from one edge of each piece, then slip it around the stem.

Carrot flies are deterred by using strips of kerosene-impregnated material in the same way as for cabbage root flies. In addition, spreading lawn mowings between rows of carrots confuses the flies.

Codling moths bore holes in apples and make the inside maggoty. Spraying is one option, but another is to tie sacking around trunks and large branches during midsummer; remove and burn it in midwinter.

Slugs and snails are destructive pests, especially during warm and wet weather. Proprietary baits can be used, but one alternative is to fill deep saucers with a mixture of beer and sugar; they are attracted to this mixture and either drown or become incapable of movement. They then can be removed and

destroyed. Make sure hedgehogs cannot reach the beer and sugar mixture.

White flies can be deterred from infesting plants by planting nasturtiums or marigolds as borders to vegetable plots.

Creating a compost heap

Recycling garden and kitchen waste into valuable material that can be dug into the ground or used as a mulch is an inexpensive technique. Grass mowings, annual weeds, soft hedge clippings, soft stems and leaves from gardens, as well as vegetable waste from kitchens, can be converted into friable, sweet-smelling material that is ideal for improving soils.

Ideally, construct three well-ventilated bins, each 1–1.1 m square and 1–1.1 m high. These are used in rotation: the first currently being filled with garden and kitchen waste; the second already filled and the material decomposing, and the third yielding well-decayed garden compost ready for use.

Making garden compost

Place the compost bins on a sheltered, well-drained piece of ground and loosely cover with straw, if available, to 23–30 cm deep. Press it down.

Form a 15 cm thick layer of garden and kitchen waste. When grass cuttings are used, make the layers thinner – thick layers compact, and exclude air. Place a 2.5–5 cm thick layer of friable soil over the first layer, thoroughly water it, and dust with sulphate of ammonia at 15g per square metre. Alternatively, a proprietary

compost activator can be used. Then, continue building up the heap, layer by layer.

When the compost heap is at the top of the container, cover with a 2.5–5 cm thick layer of friable soil. Place a sheet of thick plastic over the top to prevent the compost becoming too wet or dry. After about three months in summer (six in winter) the decayed material can

be either dug into the soil or used as a mulch.

RAISING PLANTS FROM SEED

Sowing seeds is one of the earliest signs of a settled life, a significant step in the change from a nomadic existence to one where people live in settled communities.

Seeds carry blueprints for the next generation, but for all their genetic

Left: Garden compost is easily made. Place a 15 cm thick layer of garden and kitchen waste in the base *(top left)*. Place a 5 cm thick layer of friable soil over the first layer, water it, and dust with sulphate of ammonia or a proprietary compost activator *(top right)*. Continue to fill the bin with layers of waste material *(bottom left)*. When full, place a sheet of thick plastic over the top to prevent the compost becoming too wet or dry. After about three months (longer in winter) the compost should be ready to be dug into the soil or used as a mulch *(bottom right)*.

Above: These hardy annuals have been sown in shallow V-shaped drills, with each patch of flowers sown at a slightly different angle to its neighbours. Later, the seedlings will be thinned.

complexity, they require only moisture, air and warmth to encourage germination. Most seeds need darkness to initiate germination; only a few need light. On their own, each of these needs is simple and easy to provide, but the skill in gardening is to bring all of them together at the right time. Digging beds and borders in early winter and adding bulky, organic manure or garden compost ensures that the soil is both aerated and drained, but with the ability to retain sufficient moisture to encourage germination. Winter frost, rain and snow makes surface soil crumbly and able to cloister and nurture seeds, while sowing seeds in spring, when soil is becoming warm, provides the essential warmth to initiate germination.

Adequate space for each seed is important; those grown in clusters compete for moisture and air, and although they may initially germinate, the seedlings become spindly and lank, reliant on each other for support and strength, and never develop into strong, healthy plants.

SOWING SEEDS

There are many techniques for sowing seeds, depending on whether the seeds are for ornamental or kitchen garden use.

Sowing in V-shaped drills Most vegetable seeds, as well as annual, biennial and perennial flowers, are sown in drills formed with a draw hoe. Sometimes, if the soil is very fine and only a shallow drill is needed, the end of a pointed stick is a better tool.

The first stage in sowing seeds is to rake the surface level to remove depressions and bumps. Always use a garden line to ensure the rows are straight and equally spaced; the distance between rows depends on the plants, and while carrots and scallions thrive in rows 15–23 cm apart, string beans require a spacing of 45 cm.

The depth of the V-shaped drill depends on the size of the seed, and a general indication is that the depth should be about two-and-a-half times the diameter of the seed. Therefore, drills for lettuce and scallion seeds need only be 15 mm deep, whereas those for French beans need to be about 5 cm.

Before sowing seeds, remove the garden line. Do not sow seeds directly from the packet; instead, put a few in the palm of a hand and slowly dribble them between your forefinger and thumb into

EATING WORMS AND GRUBS

There is a long history of worms being eaten, and it is recorded that epicures in France in the Middle Ages praised the taste of earthworms. People in South Africa, Japan and New Zealand, as well as more recently in America, have included worms in their diet. In New Zealand, the Maoris had a custom of reserving the eating of worms to chiefs and dying men.

The eating of grubs by the Romans was reported by Pliny, who told of grubs first being fattened on flour. The grubs of silkworms have long been a delicacy, while witchetty grubs (above) have been eaten by Aboriginals in Australia; these are the large, white grubs of several moths and longhorn beetles which infest witchetty bushes (a group of small acacias), especially the Broad-leafed Mulga.

In North America, Native Americans in the Cascade and Sierra mountains ate the larvae of Pandora moths, which normally feed upon the needles of Yellow Pines. At one stage in the moth's life it descends from trees and burrows in the soil. Slightly before this moment, Native Americans would light fires under the trees to stupefy the caterpillars, which then fell to the ground, where they were collected and either dried over a bed of hot ashes or boiled in water.

the drill. This method suits small seeds, but large ones such as beans can be individually spaced, which economizes on the amount of seed needed and removes the necessity to thin out the seedlings.

FLAT-BOTTOMED TRENCHES

Vegetables such a peas are often sown in trenches about 20 cm wide and 5 cm deep. Seeds are sown in three rows along the trench's base, and spaced 5 cm apart. This is an excellent way to grow peas in smaller gardens, and creates rows packed with pods. No thinning out of seedlings is needed.

Broadcasting On a garden scale, lawns are often created by scattering seeds over a prepared area. The soil is dug, raked level, systematically trodden to consolidate it evenly, raked again and then seed is scattered over it. Lightly rake the surface to cover the seeds.

If the soil is dry – and especially in spring and when there is little chance of rain within a few days – water the soil thoroughly, but take care that the seeds are not washed over the surface. Use string, twiggy branches, or netting to prevent birds eating the seed. Another way to prevent birds eating seeds – as well as to encourage even germination – is to cover the entire area with clear plastic. However, it must be removed when the grass seedlings are 20–25 mm high. Black plastic can also be used, but this must be removed as soon as the seeds germinate.

In groups The seeds of vegetables such as corn, beetroot, and parsnips are best sown in groups. Corn seeds are sown outdoors in spring, after all risk of frost has passed, pushing two or three seeds (each 2.5 cm apart) in groups 35 cm apart along rows 45 cm apart. After germination, thin out the seedlings to leave just one strong plant in each group.

Beetroot is also sown in groups; use a draw hoe to form V-shaped drills 20 mm deep and 30–45 cm apart. Every 10–15 cm apart along the rows, put two or three seeds. Cover the rows with a

thin layer of friable soil, and after germination, thin out the seedlings to leave the strongest young plant in each position.

Parsnips can be sown in 15–25 mm deep, V-shaped drills, but for exhibition roots use a crowbar to form a hole 75–90 cm deep. Fill it with compost, sow three seeds in each position, and after germination, thin out to leave one seedling in each position. As the parsnips don't have to struggle through rough soil, they will be beautifully shaped, and the compost will encourage good growth.

INDIAN CORN

Early North American farmers, who were equipped only with spades, shovels, mattocks, and hoes, sowed Indian Corn (Zea mays) instead of European grains, as it could be sown in fields just entirely cleared of vegetation. Additionally, maize had been grown in America for several thousand years.

Left: Garden peas can be sown in flat-bottomed trenches. Use a draw-hoe to form a trench 20 cm wide and 5 cm deep (*top left*). Scatter the seeds about 5 cm apart. Use a rake to draw soil over the seeds without disturbing them (*bottom left*). Firm the soil with the head of a rake (*bottom-right*).

THE HEALING TOUCH

*Learning to become in touch with their tactile self is an important part
of hands-on healing for many people. Some people are natural 'touchers',
and during a conversation may reach out and touch someone,
usually on an arm, shoulder or elbow.*

Clearly, this action is empathic, but it can also be a way to get to know yourself. For many people, getting to know plants through touch is a form of solace and comfort, perhaps in the same way as stroking a dog or cat. Indeed, smoothing the fur of animals is known to reduce both pulse rate and blood pressure. Many people frequently walk barefoot on carpets and lawns, and perhaps this gives reassurance and provides a greater link with nature.

The whole human body is covered with a highly sensitive sensory organ, the skin, and touch gives us detailed information about our environment and the reactions of other people. Touch can also bring security: when people feel insecure, they often wrap their arms around their body and caress their arms and shoulders. By touching plants, as well as by putting our hands in soil and potting mediums when planting new plants or repotting others, we can gain tactile comfort from gardening.

THE TOUCHING GARDEN

Many garden plants are pleasant to touch, from those with smooth, highly polished leaves to ones that are divided and soft, such as young ferns, or tougher and more resilient, like those of conifers, including the Lawson Cypress (*Chamaecyparis lawsoniana*) and the rapid-growing hybrid Leyland Cypress (× *Cupressocyparis leylandii*). In addition, some of these have aromatic leaves that offer another quality to enjoy.

The range of sensory stimuli produced by clusters of flowers, twigs, barks and stems is also extensive.

Bottlebrush-like foliage

Many pines (evergreen conifers) have stiff needles that arise from a stem and resemble a bottle cleaner. Drawing a hand along the stem, from its base to the top, produces a pleasing sensation of slight prickliness.

Prickly leaves

The common holly, *Ilex aquifolium,* as a popular, spiny-leafed shrub, an ever green with a variable nature and wide range of varieties; many garden-worthy ones have variegated leaves.

The Chinese evergreen shrub *Itea ilicifolia* has spiny-edged leaves. Similarly, the North American Oregon Grape, *Mahonia aquifolium,* sports glossy, green leaves with spiny edges.

Several junipers (evergreen conifers) have prickly, needle-like foliage, clearly

Facing page: Children have a strong desire to learn by touching everything that attracts their attention. Many children learn to love gardens by planting their own small plot.

Above center: Spiny leaves are an irresistible attraction to many people, despite the certainty of experiencing a sensation that tests reactions and the sensitivity of skin. Here is a leaf of the variegated holly *Ilex aquifolium* 'Handsworth New Silver'.

noticeable when a hand is drawn upwards and over it.

BARKS AND TWIGS

Many shrubs and trees have distinctive bark, both in colour and tactile appeal. Some have straight stems that quickly and smoothly slip through your hand, while others reveal a contorted nature.

The Yellowtwig Dogwood, *Cornus stolonifera* 'Flaviramea', has a deciduous, suckering habit, and if pruned back hard each spring to within a few centimetres of the ground it produces upright, smooth, narrow, bright greenish-yellow young shoots. In contrast, the corkscrew hazel, *Corylus avellana* 'Contorta', also known as Harry Lauder's Walking Stick, has branches curiously twisted in a spiral. It is a large, deciduous shrub. (Sir Harry Lauder was a Scottish comedian and ballad singer in vaudeville and variety halls during the late

Right: The Korean Fir, *Abies koreana,* is a large, handsome evergreen conifer with upright, cylindrical, violet-purple cones up to 8 cm long. Like many other cones, they are stimulating to touch and in no small way resemble some relaxation and stress toys that are widely sold to induce tranquillity and calmness.

Far right: Betula albosinensis 'Septentrionalis' is a form of the Chinese Red Birch that develops mainly smooth, colourful bark which creates a restful and calming sensation when touched.

BAMBOOS WITH SMOOTH LEAVES

Most bamboos have smooth, long, narrow leaves that are ideal for stroking and running through your fingers:

Black bamboo, *Phyllostachys nigra* (= *Sinarundinaria nigra*) has a gracefully arching nature. The cones are green in the first year, then jet-black.

Arrow bamboo, *Pseudosasa japonica* (= *Arundinaria japonica*) is one of the hardiest bamboos, forming dense olive-green thickets. *Sinarundinaria nitida* (= *Arundinaria nitida*), seen here, is elegant, with its narrow leaves and purple-flushed cones. Muriel bamboo, *Thamnocolamus spathaceus* (= *Arundinaria murieliae*) has cones which are initially bright green, maturing to a dull yellow-green. It is often thought to be the most graceful of all bamboos.

1800s and early 1900s whose trade-mark was a twisted walking stick.)

Trees with trunks which are interesting to stroke include the Paperbark Maple (*Acer griseum*) – a deciduous tree with papery, peeling bark – and the monkey puzzle or Chile Pine, *Araucaria araucana*, an evergreen conifer with smooth but slightly laterally ringed bark. It has the bonus of spine-tipped, stiff, overlapping leaves forming tail-like branches. The incense cedar, *Calocedrus decurrens,* is an evergreen conifer with reddish-brown, scaly, rough-textured bark. However, for an unusual trunk, densely covered with coarse, black, hairy fibres, the evergreen Chinese Windmill Palm or Chusan Palm, *Trachycorpus fortunei,* has few rivals.

Soft, woolly and hairy leaves

There are several herbaceous perennials with soft leaves that are enticing to touch. The Jerusalem Sage, *Phlomis fruticosa,* reveals grey–green, woolly leaves and is ideal in both herbaceous and mixed borders. But perhaps the best-known plant with soft leaves is Lamb's Ears, *Stachys byzantina* (earlier known as *S. lanata* and *S. olympica*). Its common

Left: The Paperbark Maple (*Acer griseum*), with its colourful bark, has great visual and tactile qualities; few people can resist touching the peeling bark.

names include Lamb's Tongue and Woolly Betony, both descriptive of the soft, hairy, oval, mid-green leaves that are smothered in white, silvery hairs. *Stachys macrantha,* with a spreading and mat-forming herbaceous habit, has hairy, mid-green leaves.

Getting to know composts and soil

Part of the therapeutic and healing value of gardening is its 'hands-on' nature in gardens, greenhouses and potting sheds. Introducing fresh life to gardens in the form of new shrubs, trees, bulbs and herbaceous perennials, as well as sowing seeds, has a rejuvenating quality that few other pastimes can offer. Even adding a

mulch around shrubs or borders can have a therapeutic value.

The range of materials used in gardening is wide, offering the opportunity for many sensory experiences.

Garden soil varies considerably from one area to another: in some it is sandy and light, in others heavy and mainly formed of clay. Potting and seed-sowing composts are either loam-based composts, consisting of friable soil with the addition of peat and sharp sand, or loam-less composts, in earlier times composed of peat, but nowadays preferably of other materials which when removed from the environment do not destroy it. All of these have distinctive qualities that can be

detected by feeling them. Indeed, composts formed of coconut fibre and coconut shells are increasingly popular, and their use does not involve damage to the environment. They are also pleasant to handle.

Mulches are formed from either organic or non-organic materials. The organic types include garden compost, peat, bark chippings, wood chippings, grass cuttings and straw. Well-decayed manure is also used, but unfortunately it is increasingly difficult to obtain. All of these organic mulches – even manure, when well-decayed! – are pleasant to touch and use.

When potting bulbs in the autumn, bulb-fibre is another material that is enjoyable to feel and work with.

Right: Soft and fleece-like seedheads have immediate appeal that encourages them to be tenderly caressed. This seedhead is from *Clematis orientalis,* a woody climber native to a wide area, from Iran to China and Korea.

Smooth and soft flower heads

These have distinctive appeal, delicate and soft to touch and magnetic to the eye. The well-known Traveller's Joy or Old Man's Beard, *Clematis vitalba,* is a vigorous, deciduous climber with silvery, glistening, umbrella-like seed heads during the autumn and throughout winter.

For creating an informal, handsome, centre-piece on a lawn, few plants can rival Pampas Grass, *Cortaderia selloana,* a perennial, evergreen grass with silvery flower plumes up to 45 cm long from late summer to late winter. These plumes are wonderful to touch and in many ways resemble feather-dusters, which few people can resist touching.

MEDICINAL STEAM BATHS

The value of steam baths has been known to Native Americans and the Maoris of New Zealand for hundreds, if not thousands, of years. During the nineteenth century, Lindesey Brine, who travelled widely in the Americas, reported that the Dakota and Chippewa Indians cured several illnesses by steam baths. They used the same methods used by the Aztecs in Mexico and Shoshones in the deserts of Utah. Wigwams about 1.2 m high were made of buffalo skins, stones heated by fire were pushed through a small opening, and water was poured over them.

In New Zealand, Maoris used steam baths to treat complaints such as rheumatism, deep bruising and skin afflictions, as well as aiding the healing of broken limbs and relieving pain after childbirth. Specific plants were added to steam baths to aid recovery.

There were several ways to do this. One was to heat several stones with fire, then to place them on a low platform over which the medicinal plant was laid. Water was poured over the stones, and a flax mat was laid over this, with the patient on top, who was enveloped in an additional, steam-retaining flax mat. Alternatively, hot stones were put into a container of water in which the medicinal plants had been steeped. The container was covered with more medicinal branches, then a flax mat, on which the patient sat, enveloped in a canopy.

The medicinal plants Maoris added to steam baths include Kahikatea (*Dacrycarpus dacrydioides,* earlier and perhaps better known as *Podocarpus dacrydioides*) to help

MEDICINAL CREAMS OR BEAUTY PREPARATIONS?

The early use of creams and other preparations is thought by anthropologists to have begun when protection from sand, wind, insects and weather was needed. Ancient Egyptians protected their bodies with coloured earths and greases; malachite green, a green mineral basically formed of copper carbonate, was used to protect eyes from strong light, and only later was it applied as a beauty treatment.

Cleopatra keenly indulged in eye decoration and painted her lower eyelids bright green and her upper lids blue, while accentuating their shape with black kohl, a finely powdered sulphide of antimony.

Painting faces continued with enthusiasm, and Elizabeth I of England whitened her face with white ceruse, a mixture of hydrate and carbonate of lead. The continual use of ceruse led to the early death of many women who used this poisonous substance.

Mud packs are well-known beauty treatments for women. Traditionally, they were made from an absorbent clay known as fuller's earth, mixed with glycerine and benzoin.

alleviate bruising. The bark and leaves of Kawakawa (*Macropiper excelsum*), also known as the Pepper Tree, were used in steam baths to excite the salivary glands, kidneys and bowels. This tree – sometimes a shrub – was a comprehensive medicine chest: its leaves were chewed to ease toothache, or softened over a fire and then used to ease boils.

Ngaio *(Myoporum laetum)*, an evergreen tree, provides twigs and leaves that, when added to steam baths, eased bruising, while branches of Koromiko (*Hebe salicifolia*) were used by women after childbirth.

Rotorua in the North Island of New Zealand is perhaps the best-known area for hot, medicinal springs. For many thousands of years their healing powers have been known to the Maoris as cures for many medical problems, including rheumatism. Often, the diet of Maoris caused constipation and haemorrhoids,

and if this happened a different type of vapour bath was used. In Rotorua, patients could lie in sulphur springs, but elsewhere there were other techniques. A small, narrow tunnel was dug into a low bank and at the far end a fire formed of chips of Totara (*Podocarpus totara*), an evergreen coniferous tree, was lit so that smoke passed along the tunnel. The patient sat on the bank and over the outlet.

Spas and hot springs

Springs are usually the natural overflow of an underground reservoir of water. The range of chemicals within spring water depends on the nature of the surrounding rock, and while most contain forms of limestone, others are rich in iron, sulphur and magnesia and are known as mineral springs.

The town of Spa, in the province of Liège, Belgium, was known in the fourteenth century for its medicinal mineral springs, and several centuries later became one of the most fashionable towns in Europe. Since then, it has given its name to other towns and cities where the waters are used medicinally.

In Britain, the bath-house in the city of Bath was constructed on the site of a spring which produced water for both drinking and bathing, and in the early eighteenth century it became fashionable for the wealthy to 'take the waters'. The springs had been known to the Romans, and in 1847 the Roman vapour baths were discovered just below the New Castle.

Baden-Baden in the Black Forest, Germany, also became a popular watering-place.

Hot springs, also known as thermal springs, are found in many regions. In North America, the Arkansas city of Hot Springs has long been a centre of health and recreation, and has many curative springs. The waters are said to be tasteless and odourless, but to contain more than twenty different chemicals with curative powers. Tradition says that these medicinal powers were known to Native Americans before the arrival of Europeans, and that Ferdinando de Soto visited them in 1541.

Another North American town, again called Hot Springs and in a valley in the Allegheny Mountains, has medicinal springs, with temperatures as high as 41°C. Other hot spring resorts in the area are Warm Sufhur Springs, Healing Springs and Jordan Alum Springs.

Above left: The long, silky plume-like flower heads of the South American Pampas Grass (*Cortaderia selloana*) create a relaxed end calming sensation when stroked.

Left: The Famous Beppu Blood Pool Hell, on the island of Kyushu, Japan. Its hot, steamy appearance adds to its mystique. Medicinal hot springs are found in many areas, and medicinal plants are often added to the water.

COLOUR HEALING IN THE GARDEN

Colour has a magical quality, strongly influencing moods and markedly contributing to our physical and mental health. Everyone has a favourite colour, and a few astrologers have long linked them with the Zodiac and personal star signs.

Colour therapy is an age-old pursuit, and was originally used in ancient Greece and in the Healing Temples of Light and Colour at Heliopolis in Egypt. The therapy was also held in high esteem by the ancient Chinese and Indians for several thousand years.

INFLUENCING OUR HEALTH

As a science, colour healing is still in its infancy, but it is clear that the colours we observe in gardens and homes, as well as those we wear, affect our health. Each colour has a personality of its own which produces an emotional response.

Pure and innocent

In the West, white is the colour of purity, and is frequently worn by brides, while in the East it is the colour of mourning. In ancient Egypt it was the colour of joy. In gardens, it has an aura of coolness and authority. White robes are particularly popular among men in Arabic countries as, unlike black, white does not absorb

light, and therefore helps to keep the wearer cool and fresh.

Calm and serene

One of the qualities associated with blue is calmness; therefore, a garden that needs to promote a sense of tranquillity should be predominantly blue. Indeed, blue is said to reduce blood pressure and to slow up the breathing and pulse rate.

Buddhists believe deep blue is the colour of infinity, and it is often thought to be the ideal colour for contemplation. In surveys of favourite colours, blue is usually the most popular, preferred by more than one-third of all people. Western religions also use blue: the Virgin

Mary is invariably depicted wearing a cloak or dress of what has come to be known as Madonna Blue.

Traditionally, hospital wards were painted white or light cream, but light blue has increasingly found favour as a colour to aid recovery.

Emotion and sexuality

Red is an emotive colour, and exposure to vermilion, in complete contrast to blue, raises blood pressure and increases the rate of respiration. It is also the colour of sexual invitation, and this, perhaps, partly accounts for the increase on pulse rate.

In India, red symbolizes great female power, sexuality and all the energy of passion and positive emotion. In China it is a lucky colour, and is worn by brides.

Cheerful and optimistic

Yellow is the colour of brightness and cheerfulness, and is claimed to be the primary colour of the intellect, hope and productivity. People who like yellow

Facing page: Borders smothered in blue flowers create a restful and tranquil ambience, helping to reduce blood pressure and to improve the quality of life.

Above: White flowers portray innocence and purity, producing an aura of tranquillity untarnished by the demands and turmoil of modern living.

are said to be individual and original in their thinking and attitude, and always willing to absorb new ideas. Strong dislike of yellow is said to indicate a rejection of introspection, a fear of innovation and, taken to its extreme, hopelessness. Incidentally, yellow is often the favourite colour of children.

Cool and soothing

Green produces a cool and soothing ambience, and signifies growth, fertility and freshness. Outdoors, shades of green vary, depending on the time of day and year and the nature of the leaf surfaces.

THE COLOUR HEALING GARDEN

Gardeners have a wide and subtle colour palette available to them, and one that is variable each day and throughout the year. Indeed, the perception of any colour changes as the intensity of light falling upon it alters. For example, light colours such as white and yellow do not lose their dominance so quickly in diminishing light as dark ones like purple and black.

Conversely, in the morning they gain their brightness quicker than dark ones.

Selecting light-coloured plants for specific places in a garden is important. For instance, positioning silver-leafed, shrubby perennials each side of the top and bottom of a flight of steps helps to make their position clear during the failing light of evening.

Border experiments

During the early eighteenth century there continued a passion for garden

Right: La Anunciacion by the Italian painter Fra Angelico (1387–1455). A Dominican friar known for religious paintings of purity and delicacy of colour, his real name was Guido de Pietro. The Madonna is invariably portrayed wearing blue, the color of tranquility.

plants in Europe as well as in North America; new plants were being found, and nurserymen and seedsmen were making them increasingly available. There was also a passion for finding new ways to use plants, and throughout the following decades – and especially in the mid- to late 1800s – gardeners experimented with them and planned both bold and subtle colour schemes.

Of all these experimenters the one now most remembered is the English garden designer Gertrude Jekyll (1843–1932). Her fame sterns from her use of colour, and it is no coincidence that early in her life she had thoughts of being a painter; however, progressive myopia led her to designing with plants. At that time, her colour schemes laid no claim to healing powers, but now many of the borders she designed offer a rich fund of ideas for the creation of gardens with a restful, sensitive and healing nature.

Selecting colours in gardens

Analyzing the qualities of colour and arranging individual colours so that their relationship can be determined has been pursued by many scientists. In North America in the latter part of the nineteenth century, A. H. Munsell defined the hue of colour as: 'the quality by which we distinguish one colour from another, as a red from a yellow, a green, a blue or a purple'. He created a colour circle formed of five principal colours (red, yellow, green, blue, purple), with intermediate colours between them.

MOURNING COLOURS

The choice of colour to indicate mourning has changed throughout the centuries and from one culture to another. In many Western civilizations, black is associated with death, but earlier, in Egypt, yellow was the colour for mourning, as it was for the Maya Indians. Yellow is also sacred to Buddha, and in India is believed to bring luck; the Chinese distinguished important people with a yellow coat.

In Christian Germany in the fifteenth century, yellow was said to be offensive to God, resulting in its complementary colours, violet and purple, being appropriated as symbols of mourning and redemption.

In Brittany, as well as earlier in Persia (now Iran), brown was the colour of mourning – the colour of falling leaves in the autumn.

During the latter part of the fifteenth century, Queen Anne, the wife of Charles VIII of France, introduced black as the colour of mourning, instead of white.

Secluded areas of leafy, green trees have long played a healing role, as well as creating a contemplative ambience. Like other colours, the perceived tone of green also varies depending on the intensity of light. If the surface is smooth, a large proportion of light is reflected, which makes the perceived light purer and brighter. The surface of some leaves is matte and does not reflect the same amount of light, so they appear dull.

Left: In the autumn, many deciduous trees and shrubs create a feast of colour before their leaves fall.

Other scientists had earlier contributed to colour research, and in the late seventeenth century the English scientist Sir Isaac Newton (1642–1727) produced a colour wheel with seven colours (red, orange, yellow, green, blue, indigo, violet). Other colour circles have consisted of four colours (red, yellow, green, blue), while the one now most commonly used has three. These are red, yellow and blue, with three secondary colours (orange, green and violet).

Another idea for a colour wheel came from the *Irish Farmer's Gazette* in the mid-1800s (shown on facing page).

Using colour wheels Colour wheels have been used by scientists for hundreds of years. The colours used in these wheels have differed, but their prime value to gardeners lies in choosing both complementary and harmonizing colours.

Complementary types do not have any common colour, so they create strong contrasts. They are found on opposite sides of a colour wheel.

Harmonizing types share the same colours and are found close together on a colour wheel. They create a restful ambience in the garden.

The simplest colour wheel uses three main colours (red, blue, yellow); where they overlap, additional colours are created. For example, green is produced by yellow and blue, violet by red and blue, and orange by yellow and red.

For dramatic colour contrasts in gardens, choose complementary colours – for example, yellow vividly contrasts with red or violet. For subtle and restful arrangements, choose harmonizing hues, such as blue and green.

To gain an appreciation of Munsell's colour circle, take a strip of paper about 2.5 cm wide and mark it into ten equal parts. In each section, write in the

COLOUR ABSORPTION

When sunlight falls upon coloured surfaces some of the colours present in white light are absorbed by the colour of the surface and are not reflected. This is known as colour absorption and makes primary colours, such as yellow, red and blue, more dominant. This illustration shows the result of sunlight falling on a yellow tulip.

Right: Red is a dramatic colour and can create a confused image when intermingled with green. Here, however, red tulips have been planted among contrasting 'White Dame' wallflowers.

following colours in this order on both sides of the paper: red, red–yellow, yellow, yellow–green, green, green–blue, blue, blue–purple, purple, purple–red. Then, form the strip into a circle (left).

COLOUR-THEME GARDENS

Creating gardens or borders predominantly of one colour, and thereby influencing health, is easy. The range of plants to choose from is wide, and includes shrubs, trees, bulbs, annuals and herbaceous perennials. By using a medley of different types of plants it is possible to have specific colours throughout most of summer, and by using conifers and evergreen shrubs and trees, to carry the theme throughout winter.

However, it would be very restrictive to confine specific colour-themed borders solely to those that reflect the main theme: a few harmonizing colours thinly peppered among them helps in a subtle way to reinforce the colour theme, as well as often extending the flowering season. On this and following pages a few plants are suggested to form colour-theme borders.

White and silver borders

With their purity and brightness, white flowers have both a dramatic and subdued effect: in strong summer sunlight they have an immediate and often penetrating quality, while during the diminishing light of evening they are less forceful.

Silver is less dominant than white, and is usually defined as a lustrous greyish-

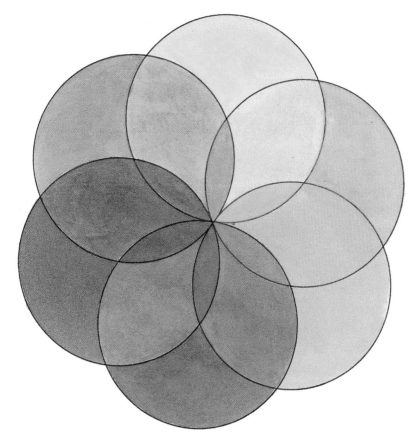

white or whitish-grey. Its silver nature, reflecting light at many angles, has a variable but dull sparkle not seen in pure white. Also, it is more often seen in leaves than flowers.

Grey borders – formed of silver- and grey-foliaged plants, with flowers a medley of white, lilac, purple and pink – are usually as their best in late summer and into early autumn.

Here are a few plants to consider for a white-and-silver border:

Trees and shrubs Many create a wealth of white and silver flowers, while others are better known for their silvery leaves.

One of the most spectacular spring-flowering shrubs, sometimes a tree, is the North American Snowy Mespilus, *Amelanchier lamarckii* (also known as June Berry, Shad Bush and Sugar Plum). Its white, starlike flowers are borne in clouds, with the bonus of tinted foliage in autumn.

The Kousa, *Cornus kousa chinensis*, is another hardy, deciduous shrub, with purplish-green flowers surrounded by four dominant, white bracts during midsummer. The Chilean *Eucryphia glutinosa*, a deciduous or partially evergreen, tree-like shrub, reveals large, white flowers and masses of stamens with

Above left: This complex colour wheel appeared in the *Irish Farmer's Gazette* in the mid 1800s, confirming the interest in the science of light and colour more than 100 years ago.

WEDDING BLUES!

Blue is claimed to be the colour of Venus, the ancient Roman goddess of gardens and spring, as well as the goddess of love and beauty. Blue has long been associated in folklore with weddings and brides, but many of these sayings contradict each other. The most common saying suggests that on her wedding day a bride should wear:

Something old,
Something new,
Something borrowed,
Something blue.

yellow anthers during mid- and late summer. Better known is the Hills of Snow or Sevenbark, *Hydrangea arborescens,* a hardy and deciduous shrub from North America, with large heads of white flowers during mid- and late summer. The variety 'Grandiflora' has larger clusters of pure white flowers.

The Star Magnolia, *Magnolia stellata,* is a deciduous tree or shrub ideal in borders or as a feature alongside a lawn. In mid-spring it develops white, starlike flowers about 10 cm across.

Widely known as either the Bridal Wreath or Foam of May, *Spiraea × arguta* is a hardy, deciduous shrub that creates a mass of pure-white flowers during mid- and late spring.

Gardens in late spring and early summer can be dominated by the large, rounded heads of snow-white flowers borne on the hardy and deciduous shrub *Viburnum opulus* 'Sterile', widely and aptly known as the Snowball Bush.

The most spectacular shrub with silver or grey foliage is the evergreen *Brachyglottis greyi* (earlier and more popularly known as *Senecio greyi* and S. *laxifolius*). It has a broad, domed outline smothered in silvery-grey leaves. During midsummer it produces yellow, daisy-like flowers. The Willow-leafed Pear, *Pyrus salicifolia* 'Pendula', is a deciduous tree with narrow, silver-grey leaves and the bonus of white flowers in mid- and late spring.

Border flowers There is a wealth of these plants, some with white flowers, others

revealing silvery leaves. The hardy, herbaceous Pearly Everlasting or Life Everlasting, *Anaphalis margaritacea yedoensis* (earlier known as *A. yedoensis*), has clustered heads of white flowers from midsummer to early autumn. Another herbaceous perennial known by the same common names is *Anaphalis triplinervis*. It develops narrow, silvery-gray leaves and white flowers in late summer.

For a wealth of silvery-grey leaves, *Artemisia absinthium* 'Lambrook Silver' has few rivals. It is deciduous and shrubby, with yellow flowers during mid- and late summer. The White Sage, *Artemisia ludoviciana,* is a hardy, North American, herbaceous perennial also known as Western Mugwort and Cudweed. It is covered in deeply divided, woolly, white leaves, and has silvery-white flowers during late summer and into early autumn.

Baby's Breath, *Gypsophila paniculata*, is a hardy, herbaceous perennial also known as Chalk Plant and Gauze Flower. During summer it produces clouds of white flowers.

Botanists are always changing plant names, and the Shasta Daisy is a hardy, herbaceous perennial that has suffered in

HEDGES FOR BACKGROUND COLOUR

Traditionally, flower borders were backed by hedges, and the choice of plant for these much depended on the colour theme:

Gray borders are superb when backed by *Tamarix gallica* (French Tree or Manna Plant), with feathery, grey-green foliage.

Yellow and gold borders can be backed by yew, *Taxus baccata*, but a variation is yellow-and-green variegated hollies.

Orange, blue and green, borders are best backed by yew hedges, which create a deep, glossy backdrop to plants.

Facing page: The perceived colour intensity of silver-leafed borders changes dramatically depending on the intensity of light falling on them. Strong sunlight gives them sparkle and vibrancy, whereas in shade or low light some silver plants assume shades of dull green.

Left: Green-leafed hedges create a restful background colour for many garden plants. Here, the hedge both provides a background and forms a serpentine that helps to create an unusual and visually stimulating garden.

BIT OF A SWEAT

The North American Bull Bay or Southern Magnolia, Magnolia grandiflora, *a large, evergreen tree, has bark used by Native Americans as a tonic and to induce sweating.*

Above right: Few evergreen shrubs are as dramatic as the North American Bull Bay or Southern Magnolia, *Magnolia grandiflora.* Its bowl-shaped, fragrant flowers are up to 20 cm across and appear from midsummer to autumn.

this way. It is now properly known as *Leucanthemum maximum,* but earlier and more popularly as *Chrysanthemum maximum.* It is also known as Max Daisy and Daisy Chrysanthemum, and has large, white, daisy-like flowers up to 8 cm wide during mid- and late summer.

Senecio cineraria has also been subject to a number of name changes, and was earlier known as *Senecio bicolor* and *Cineraria maritima.* It is a half-hardy perennial with leaves smothered in white, woolly hairs. The variety 'Diamond' has deeply divided leaves. Another plant rebaptized repeatedly by botanists is Lamb's Tongue; it is now known as *Stachys byzantina,* but earlier as *S. lanata* and *S. olympica.* It is herbaceous, with leaves smothered in white, silvery hairs.

The Ornamental Thistle, *Onopordum acanthium* (also known as Scotch Thistle, Silver Thistle, Gentine Thistle and Giant Thistle), is an essential part of silver borders. It is a hardy biennial with silvery-grey, jaggedly lobed leaves.

The Californian Tree Poppy, *Romneya coulteri* (also known as Californian Tree Poppy and Matilija Poppy), is a spectacular shrubby and herbaceous perennial with 10–12.5 cm wide white flowers that reveal yellow centres.

YELLOW AND GOLD BORDERS

Borders of these colours are radiant and dominant, especially when sunlight is strong. Yellow flowers are at their best in summer, although there is a splattering of them throughout the year.

Trees and shrubs

Acer shirasawanum 'Aureum' (earlier known as *A. japonicum* 'Aureum'), is a hardy, deciduous, bushy tree with bright-yellow, maple-like leaves and ideal for planting in a lawn. Darwin's Berberis, *Berberis darwinii,* however, is a hardy, evergreen shrub famed for its drooping clusters of deep-orange-yellow flowers during late spring and early summer.

The Golden Indian Bean Tree, *Catalpa bignonioides* 'Aurea', is a deciduous tree with large, heart-shaped, yellow leaves. In midsummer it develops purple and yellow, foxglove-like flowers. But for year-round colour, the yellow foliaged evergreen *Chamaecyparis lawsoniana* 'Lutea' has few peers. *Cupressus macrocarpa* 'Goldcrest' is another yellow foliaged evergreen conifer; it is ideal for forming a hedge.

Winter need not be bare of yellow flowers; the Cornelian Cherry, *Cornus mas* (also known as Sorbet), is a hardy, deciduous, bushy shrub with clusters of golden-yellow flowers borne on naked branches from late winter to mid-spring.

The Chinese Witch Hazel, *Hamamelis mollis,* is another deciduous shrub or small tree with winter flowers. Spider-like, yellow flowers are borne on bare branches during winter and early spring.

The hardy, deciduous shrub *Forsythia × intermedia* is a certain harbinger of spring, with masses of golden-yellow, bell-shaped flowers. The Double-flowered Gorse, *Ulex europaeus* 'Plenus', is also spring-flowering, although the flowers continue into early summer, and often intermittently to autumn. The pea-shaped, golden-yellow flowers are borne amid spiny stems.

The deciduous Spanish Gorse or Spanish Broom, *Genista hispanica*, has a spiny nature, with masses of golden-yellow, pea-shaped flowers during early and midsummer.

Hypericum 'Hidcote', a hardy, semi-evergreen shrub (also known as *H. patulum* 'Hidcote'), creates a spectacular display of large, saucer-shaped, golden-yellow flowers from mid- or late summer to autumn.

The deciduous shrub, *Kerria japonica* 'Pleniflora', has a lax nature, with arching stems bearing bright orange-yellow flowers in spring and early summer.

The Shrubby Cinquefoil, *Potentilla* 'Elizabeth', a hardy, deciduous shrub, is one of the longest-flowering shrubs, with canary-yellow flowers from early summer to early autumn.

The Yellow Locust, *Robinia pseudoacacia* 'Frisia' (also known as False Acacia and Black Locust), is a hardy, deciduous tree with golden-yellow foliage. It is ideal for planting in a lawn.

Border flowers

The range of yellow-flowered herbaceous plants is wide. The Fern-leaf Yarrow, *Achillea filipendulina*, has large, platelike heads of lemon-yellow flowers during mid- and late summer. The variety 'Coronation Gold' reveals deep-yellow flowers. For a dainty herbaceous

Left: Green is an accommodating colour that harmonizes with most other colours, especially the yellow-flowered – but not dominant – santolina in the foreground.

HEALING WOUNDS

Earlier known as Goldrufe,
Aaron's Rod and
Woundwort, Solidago
virgaurea *was highly valued*
for healing wounds,
internally and externally.
The leaves are used to make a
tea, as well as a poultice for
wounds. In addition, the
roots and leaves were used as
a mild sedative and to treat
digestive upsets.

perennial, the Lady's Mantle, *Alchemilla mollis,* has few rivals. With light-green, shallowly lobed leaves and masses of tiny, sulphur-yellow, star-shaped flowers in frothy sprays from early to late summer, it creates a wonderful display alongside paths.

Tickseed, *Coreopsis verticillata,* has a herbaceous perennial nature, with finely divided leaves and bright-yellow, starlike flowers which bloom from early summer to early autumn.

Although a perennial, the California Poppy, *Eschscholzia californica,* is usually grown as a hardy annual. It develops finely cut leaves and masses of bright orange-yellow flowers from early summer to the autumn.

For a display of deep yellow flowers throughout summer, the Garden Loosestrife or Yellow Loosestrife, *Lysimachia punctata,* is the hardy, herbaceous plant to choose.

The Jerusalem Sage, *Phlomis fruticosa,* is a shrubby evergreen with whorls of yellow flowers during early and mid-summer.

Rudbeckia fulgida, a coneflower, is a North American hardy, herbaceous perennial with yellow to orange flowers, each with a purple-brown, conelike centre, from mid- to late summer. There are several superb varieties.

The Black-eyed Susan, *Rudbeckia hirta,* again from North America, is a

short-lived perennial usually grown as a hardy annual, with masses of golden-yellow flowers during late summer and into autumn.

The Globe Flower, *Trollius × cultorum,* is a handsome, hardy, herbaceous perennial, with large, pale-yellow to orange, globe-shaped flowers during late spring and early summer. There are many superb varieties.

BLUE AND PURPLE BORDERS

Borders formed mainly of these colours are not at their best until the start of summer. There are, of course, exceptions and the rosy purple, late winter-flowering *Rhododendron × praecox* is an example. But once the blue theme is under way in summer, it can continue right into autumn with the Michaelmas Daisy, *Aster novae angliae* (known in North America as New England Aster). The name Michaelmas Daisy comes from

FLOWERING HEDGES FOR CHANGING COLOUR

The foliage colour of deciduous hedges slowly changes throughout the year: in spring, young, light-coloured shoots appear, darkening as summer progresses. But it is the flowering ones that reveal the most dramatic changes.

Hedges formed of forsythia, a deciduous shrub, create a sudden impact of bright-yellow flowers in spring. Then, fresh green leaves appear, later darkening before falling in autumn. *Forsythia × intermedia* is good for forming a hedge.

The Bridal Wreath or Foam of May, *Spiraea × arguta,* produces masses of white flowers during mid- and late spring, together with fresh young leaves, darkening slightly and persisting through to the autumn.

The Shrubby Cinquefoil, *Potentilla fruticosa,* creates a low hedge with yellow flowers that persist throughout summer. As the flowers diminish in late summer, the finely lobed, mid-green leaves become more apparent.

the plant's ability to flower on Michaelmas Day, 29 September, as well as on the old date of this quarter day, 10 October, in earlier days an important time in the agricultural calendar.

Blue-themed borders are attractive and can be enhanced by adding patches of dull-white and pale-lemon flowers, but not strong yellows, which are bound to dominate the border, especially when in strong sunlight.

The range of blue- and purple-flowered herbaceous plants is wide, but there are a few shrubs, trees and conifers to consider too.

Trees and shrubs

Blue foliage creates a dramatic effect in borders, but take care with purple-leafed shrubs, as when used in excess they can be too dominant. Also, in the diminishing light of evening they can excessively darken a border.

The Purple-leafed Filbert, *Corylus maxima* Purpurea', is a dramatic, hardy, deciduous shrub, with large, somewhat heart-shaped, rich-purple leaves. For another deciduous shrub with deep-purple leaves, try *Cotinus coggygria* 'Notcutt's Variety'. Less dramatic, the evergreen conifer Koster's Blue Spruce, *Picea pungens* 'Koster', has intensely blue foliage, but is not dominant. *Picea pungens* 'Thomsén' reveals pale silvery-blue foliage.

With long, lax spires, up to 20 cm long, of powder-blue flowers, *Ceanothus* 'Gloire de Versailles' creates a superb display from midsummer to early autumn. It

is hardy and deciduous. Of quite a different nature, the deciduous Judas Tree or Love Tree, *Cercis siliquastrum*, has a round-headed but spreading nature, with stunning clusters of rich, rose-purple flowers on bare branches in the late spring and early summer.

The Common Hydrangea, *Hydrangea macrophylla* (also known as French Hydrangea and Hortensia), is a hardy, deciduous shrub with a rounded outline which flowers during mid- and late summer. There are two forms of this shrub: Hortensia types have large, globose heads,

Facing page, above: Many herbaceous asters, such as *Aster amellus* 'King George', have bright blue flowers which create dominant displays in herbaceous and mixed borders.

Facing page, below: Forsythia hedges are dramatic in spring, when yellow flowers create vitality and proclaim the departure of winter. This is *Forsythia × intermedia* 'Lynwood'.

Left: Spring-flowering bulbs growing in pots create medleys of colour in conservatories or sunrooms where the temperature is not too high. These hyacinths, irises and narcissi make good use of the dramatic contrast of blue and bright yellow.

RED FRUITS

During autumn many shrubs and trees produce stunningly attractive red fruits; some persist through to spring. Cotoneaster *'Cornubia' has large, red fruits;* Malus *'Red Sentinel' has cardinal-red fruits that often persist to spring.*

Sorbus aucuparia *'Asplenifolia' has deeply cut, fernlike leaves that assume red tints in the autumn and also produces scarlet berries.*

while Lacecaps have flatter formations and a less dense appearance. There are several blue varieties.

With a lower stance, the French Lavender or Spanish Lavender, *Lavandula stoechas*, is a hardy, evergreen shrub with narrow, grey-green leaves and deep-purple flowers in early and midsummer.

Border flowers

These are mainly of a herbaceous nature, and create spectacular displays year after year. The well-known monkshood, *Aconitum napellus* (also known as Wolf's Bane and Helmet Flower), develops hoodlike, deep-blue flowers during mid- and late summer. A related plant, *Aconitum wilsonii*, has deeply divided leaves and lax spires of

amethyst-blue flowers during late summer and into the autumn. There are several good varieties.

Most African Lilies have a slightly tender nature, but *Agapanthus* 'Headbourne Hybrids' is hardier than most and has a bulbous nature with umbrella-like heads of deep-violet-blue to pale-blue flowers during mid- and late summer.

Alkanet or Italian Bugloss, *Anchusa azurea*, is a hardy, herbaceous perennial with upright stems bearing lax arrays of bright-blue flowers from early to late summer.

Herbaceous asters are well known and include *Aster sediformis* (earlier known as *A. acris*). It develops masses of lavender-blue flowers with golden centres during late summer and into the autumn. Another aster, *Aster amellus* 'King George', develops

large, violet-blue, daisy-like flowers with golden-yellow centres in late summer and early autumn.

The North American *Camassia quamash* (commonly known as camass, comosh and quamash), is a hardy, herbaceous, bulbous perennial with clusters of blue to purple flowers during early and midsummer.

Delphinium elatum is a well-known herbaceous perennial; there are two forms, in colours including lavender, mauve, blue and white.

The Purple Cone Flower, *Echinacea purpurea*, is hardy and herbaceous, with large, purple-crimson flowers from midsummer to autumn.

The Globe Thistle, *Echinops ritro*, is a distinctive herbaceous perennial with globular, steel-blue flower heads during mid- and late summer. With a similar nature, fleabane, *Erigeron speciosus*, has daisy-like, purple flowers from early to late summer. There are many excellent varieties.

The North American Joe Pye Weed, *Eupatorium purpureum* (also known as Sweet Joe Pye Weed and Green-stemmed Joe Pye Weed), has a hardy, herbaceous perennial nature and develops large heads packed with rose-purple flowers during late summer. Meadowsweet, *Filipendula purpurea*, has a similar nature, with large heads of small carmine-rose flowers during midsummer.

With a slightly different nature, the tuberous-rooted Blazing Star, *Liatris spicata* (also known as Gayfeathers and Button

Right: The cormous-rooted crocosmia produces dominant mounds of colour during mid- and late summer. There are many varieties to choose from, including 'Carmin Brilliant' with its masses of red flowers.

Snakeroot), develops paintbrush-like heads of pinkish-purple flowers during late summer and early autumn.

For flowers with originality, the Obedience Plant, Lion's Head, or False Dragonhead, *Physostegia virginiana,* has few rivals. It is a hardy, herbaceous perennial with long spires of tubular, pink-mauve flowers during mid- and late summer. Each flower, when pushed to one side, will remain in position.

Jacob's Ladder or Greek Valerian, *Polemonium folisissimum,* is a North American hardy, herbaceous perennial with mauve-blue flowers in clustered heads from early to late summer. With a similar herbaceous nature, spiderwort,

Tradescantia virginiana 'Isis', creates triangular, three-petalled, royal-blue flowers from early to late summer.

RED AND PINK BORDERS

Reds are dramatic colours and can soon dominate borders; pinks, however, which are desaturated reds, have a gentle aura that does not dazzle the eye, especially when in strong sunlight.

The perceived shade of red dramatically changes during the diminishing light of evening until, when practically all light has gone, they almost become black. Pink, however, remains discernible long after strong reds have merged with their background.

Above: Forget-me-nots (*myosotis*) are frequently planted as a narrow edging to borders, but create more drama when planted in a wide border. This irregular pattern of shades of blue creates a restful but interesting ambience.

COLOURED DECKING

Paths and patios should harmonize with the garden, and while many old and natural paving materials achieved this, some modern materials have a garish and dominant nature. Brightly coloured paving around swimming pools is often acceptable, but when used in a checked pattern to create a large patio, it too often results in the area dominating the entire garden at the expense of plants.

Reds are available throughout the year, through flower colours, barks and stems, berries or as autumn colour, when many deciduous trees develop vividly coloured leaves.

Trees and shrubs

The best-known shrub with red foliage is the superbly attractive *Acer palmatum* 'Dissectum Atropurpureum'. It is hardy and deciduous, with a domed outline smothered in finely cut, bronze-red leaves throughout summer.

The range of flowering trees and shrubs, however, is wide and includes *Azalea* 'Kirin', a hardy, evergreen azalea which in spring becomes smothered in deep-rose-coloured flowers. There are many other red and pink varieties.

The Chilean Fire Bush or Chilean Fire Tree, *Embothrium coccineum,* is an

HEALING WOUNDS

The ubiquitous daisy, Bellis
perennis *(earlier known as
bruisewort), is widely seen in
lawns throughout summer.
However, it has a long
history of reducing bruising
and staunching the flow of
blood from wounds.
Herbalists say that leaves
pounded to a pulp and
stirred into melted cream or
butter, with the addition of
cayenne pepper, create an
effective salve.*

evergreen tree with an upright habit and brilliant orange-scarlet flowers during early and midsummer. It prefers warm, sunny regions. The Shrubby Mallow, *Hibiscus syriacus* 'Woodbridge' (also known as Althaea and Shrub Althaea), is hardier, forming a deciduous shrub with 8 cm wide, rose-pink flowers in mid-and late summer and often into early autumn. It is ideal for introducing colour to borders in the latter part of summer.

The North American Calico Bush, *Kalmia latifolia* (also known as Mountain Laurel, Spoonwood and Ivybush), is an exceedingly beautiful evergreen shrub. During early summer it develops clusters of bowl-shaped, bright-pink flowers. With a common name like Beauty Bush, *Kolkwitzia amabilis* is assured of success in

a border. It has a hardy, deciduous nature with arching branches bearing pink, foxglove-like flowers with yellow throats during late spring and early summer. The variety 'Pink Cloud' has clear-pink flowers.

The deciduous shrub Flowering Nutmeg, *Leycesteria formosa* (also known as Granny's Curls, Himalaya Honeysuckle and Pheasant Berry), has two attractive qualities; in mid- and late summer it develops white flowers surrounded by dark claret bracts, followed by purplish-red berries in the autumn.

For a spectacular display, the deciduous shrub *Magnolia liliiflora* 'Nigra' has few equals. During late spring and early summer it develops 8 cm high, deep-reddish-purple flowers. Ideal for lime-

free soils, *Pieris japanica* 'Blush', a hardy evergreen shrub, has pale-blush-pink flowers in spring.

Weigela hybrids, with their hardy, deciduous nature, never fail to create attractive displays. During late spring and early summer they produce a wealth of honeysuckle-shaped flowers. There is a wide range of varieties, including: 'Abel Carriere' (deep-rose-carmine with a yellow throat) and 'Newport Red' (dark red).

Border flowers

There are many herbaceous perennials to choose from. The Common Bear's Breeches or Artist's Acanthus, *Acanthus mollis,* develops tall, upright spires of white and purple flowers during mid- and late summer.

Alstroemeria aurantiaca, the Peruvian Lily or Lily of the Incas, is a tuberous rooted herbaceous perennial with trumpet-shaped, rich orange to orange scarlet flowers during mid- and late summer. With a cormous nature, the hardy montbretia, *Crocosmia masonorum,* develops flame-orange flowers from mid- to late summer. There are several varieties, including: 'Bressingham Blaze' (orange-red), 'Emberglow' (orange-red) and 'Vulcan' (orange-red).

The hardy, herbaceous perennial, Bleeding Heart, *Dicentra spectabilis,* is a well-known border plant, with dainty stems bearing rose-red, heart-shaped flowers during early summer. A white variety is also available.

Right: Pink themed borders
have a soft, warm, friendly
ambience that immediately
gives them a romantic
character.

Hemerocallis 'Pink Damask', a hardy, herbaceous perennial, develops stiff, upright stems bearing pink flowers with yellow throats mainly during early and midsummer. There are several other red and pink varieties. However, for a blaze of red, the Red Hot Poker, *Kniphofia* (also known as Flame Flower, Poker Plant and Torch Lily), has few peers. It is a herbaceous perennial with distinctive poker-like heads from midsummer to autumn, with a wide range of red-flowered varieties.

As its common name Cardinal Flower implies, *Lobelia cardinalis* has brilliant scarlet flowers. These appear during mid- and late summer on this short-lived, hardy, herbaceous perennial. The Purple Loosestrife or Spiked Loosestrife, *Lythrum salicaria,* is longer living, with a hardy, herbaceous nature. From midsummer to early autumn it bears tightly clustered reddish-purple flowers.

The North American Perennial or Fall Phlox, *Phlox paniculata,* is a hardy,

herbaceous perennial with masses of flowers during mid- and late summer. The colour range is wide and includes pink and red varieties.

The Crimson Flag, *Schizostylis coccinea,* is another herbaceous perennial with a common name that indicates the colour of its flowers – rich crimson – borne in autumn.

COLOUR HARMONIES AND CONTRASTS ON PATIOS

The colour of a wall of a patio has a marked influence.

White walls have a clinical nature. Yellow, gold and scarlet flowers, as well as green foliage, suit them.

SPRING DISPLAYS:
Blue forget-me-nots and golden wallflowers; Daisies (*Bellis perennis*) and red wallflowers; blue and red hyacinths.

SUMMER DISPLAYS:
Geraniums, marigolds, calceolarias, tagetes, petunias and zinnias.

Grey stone walls create a restful, undemanding ambience. Select mainly deep-purple, deep-blue, pink or red flowers.

SPRING DISPLAYS:
Red wallflowers, blue forget-me-nots, and pink tulips; pink or blue hyacinths; polyanthus.

SUMMER DISPLAYS:
Petunias and calceolorias; Blue lobelia and scarlet geraniums; Star of Bethlehem (*Campanula isophylla*), stocks, heliotropes and nasturtiums.

Red brick walls are dominant and often need flowers and foliage to soften their strong colour. Colours to choose are mainly white, soft blue, silver, and lemon.

SPRING DISPLAYS:
Blue forget-me-nots and white hyacinths; bronze and cream wallflowers and pink and white daisies (*Bellis perennis*); grape hyacinths (*Muscari armeniacum*) and white tulips; blue polyanthus and small-leafed variegated ivies.

SUMMER DISPLAYS:
Stocks; Sweet Alyssum (*Lobularia maritima*); blue stocks and *Senecio cineraria* 'Diamond'.

Above left: The late-spring and early-summer flowering *Weigela* creates festoons of honeysuckle-shaped flowers.

Left: Scented pelargoniums introduce colour and fragrance to patios. *Pelargonium graveolens* has the bouquet of roses; there are several other fragrant-leafed types. The subtle colours soften the dominance of the brick wall.

HEALING PATTERNS, FORMS, SHAPES AND SCULPTURES

Early Man throughout the world was concerned with patterns and shapes, and left a legacy of stone monuments and earthworks that hold memorial, social or religious values.

Creating patterns and shapes has also captivated gardeners, usually using plants such as trees and shrubs to produce permanent patterns. Ephemeral designs have also been formed, using annual plants in summer bedding displays. These were popularized through 'carpet bedding' in England during the 1800s, also known as tapestry bedding, mosaic bedding and jewel bedding. Motifs, as well as intricate patterns, were soon part of the annual competition to surpass neighbouring and national displays.

THE PHILOSOPHY OF PATTERN THERAPY

Shapes and patterns are claimed to have a marked influence on our lives and to, have value in helping to cure diseases and to alleviate psychological problems. Not everyone is immediately sensitive to the auras said to be created by pattern therapy, but it is claimed that we all can cultivate and develop these powers, which are of a spiritual and supersensory

nature. Much of this sensitivity to shapes is described in ancient writings dating back several thousand years from China, Tibet, India, Japan and Egypt. Indeed, pyramid healing – where the proportions of pyramids create harmony with nature – is claimed to harness electromagnetic forces and to benefit health and aid healing.

The shapes of many things in our everyday lives are also said to have an influence, and a yogurt manufacturer has

claimed that a newly designed container increased the activity of bacteria, while schizophrenic patients are said to improve dramatically when moved to trapezoidally shaped wards. Also, it is claimed injured mice in spherical cages recover more quickly.

In gardens

It is not just the shape of a building that has curative powers, but also its contents and their positions. Feng shui, also known as *kan yu,* is an ancient Chinese version of geomancy, and uses the 'cosmic breath' or 'vital spirit' that runs through the earth to influence the good fortune of individuals living there.

Ideally, a dwelling should face south and be positioned two-thirds of the way up a hill, be on dry land, and have slight hills to the east and west. Water plays an important role, and this should gather in a pond below the dwelling. Clearly, in this congested world, few houses and gardens can expect to fulfil all or indeed

Facing page: Clipped Box, *Buxus sempervirens,* combined with a Japanese-type statue, creates a medley of shapes and textures that retains attention in a restful manner.

Above centre: During the mid- to late 1800s the enthusiasm far carpet bedding created many ambitious and attractive displays. The pattern shown here appeared in the *Gardener's Chronical* in 1877.

55

Right: This Japanese garden has large stepping stones with a wide, ribbon-like strip of coloured, shalelike pebbles alongside and crossing to simulate the movement of a stream. Other pebbles, as well as gravel, are used to create other shapes and colour-contrasting areas.

Below: The ability of water to both capture and direct attention in gardens was recognized as early as during the Roman Empire. Here a river isolates one part of the garden from another in Devonshire in the early 1800s. The bridge allows access to the temple-like building on the hill.

corners, and especially not where several straight roads converge.

To deflect evil spirits entering a Chinese garden, screens (known as 'spirit walls') are built to face entrances in outside walls, preserving peace and retaining good influences. Inside the garden, winding walls also concentrate good luck. Old, perhaps contorted, trees are invaluable for attracting and harbouring the cosmic wind; water also acts as a reservoir for good fortune, and is especially beneficial when several small pools flow into a larger one.

see into the distance, it produces a hopeful and uplifting ambience, whereas when curtain-like and restrictive a depressive aura is created – one that favours illness and depression.

Formal and clinically designed gardens – with neat hedges and paths and plants in geometric patterns – produce a sense of unity and regimentation. Informal gardens, however – where paths meander and borders are a medley of herbaceous perennials, annuals, bulbs, shrubs and small trees – have a soft and friendly appearance that encourages relaxation and healing.

any of these demands, but the philosophy still remains good.

Gentle curves that follow the natural landscape are preferred to straight lines, which are claimed to give easy travel to evil spirits. In towns and cities, entrances must not be at the ends of streets or near

INFLUENCING MOODS

The shapes and styles of gardens influence our lives. In addition, the background of a garden has a marked bearing on our welfare, especially when someone is recovering from an illness. If the background is open, allowing the eye to

Creating focal points

Attracting the eye to a feature at the end of a garden helps to remove introspection and to create a feeling of openness and looking to the future. Plants, statues and garden buildings can be used.

Flowering trees, as well as those with variegated or autumn-coloured foliage, create attractive focal points; large and distinctive yellow-leafed conifers are especially attractive and form points of interest throughout the year, whereas a display of flowering and foliage trees is limited. Even in winter and when a garden is covered in snow, the simple but distinctive outline of a yellow conifer looks superb.

If there is an attractive view beyond the end of your garden, either frame it with distinctive conifers on each side of the garden's end, or put a small group of trees of varying sizes and shapes to one side. Plan this display so that the outline slopes down on the side of the garden where the view continues.

Summerhouses, positioned at a slight angle and with a tall, coloured conifer on one side, can also be used to define the garden's end and to direct the eye to features beyond. However, if the building is positioned directly facing the house, it immediately closes off the garden. This, of course, may be necessary where other gardens abut the end of your plot.

Statues play a role in creating focal points, but need to be positioned carefully and with suitably sized plants behind them if their visual impact is not to be diminished. For example, a tall statue, when backed by a yew hedge some 2 m high, appears dominant and attractive. The dark green of the hedge highlights the white nature of most statues. But if the background is one of variously coloured trees about 4 m high, the visual dominance of the statue is lost except when seen at close quarters. Before buying any statue, always visualize its position in your garden, together with its background and the distance from which it will usually be seen.

Healing hedges

Hedges, originally used to protect gardens from vagrant animals and intruders,

Above left: Statues in clipped recesses in hedges and framed by narrow, upright conifers create dramatic features that are eye-catching throughout the year.

Right This narrow path, canopied by a pergola clothed in leafy and flowering climbers, immediately directs attention to an urn and pedestal that are highlighted by the dark-leafed hedge.

Facing page: From this perspective the statue of Pan snugly fits into an arch formed by a yew hedge. Statues add interest to gardens throughout the year and can be especially attractive when low rays of sunlight glance upon them during winter and spring.

have become ornamental features, with both foliage and flowering plants being used. They also play a vital role in a healing garden, where backgrounds of flowers or attractive foliage help to cloister people who are seriously ill until they are able to experience more open aspects and look forward to total recovery.

Hedges also play a role in feng shui, directing the flow of beneficial spirits and preventing entry of evil ones into gardens.

Hedges can be used both at boundaries and within the garden. Clearly, those for a garden's perimeter need to be hardy, able to create privacy, and be more resistant to wind than internal types, which are usually decorative and smaller.

Boundary hedges Cottage garden hedges of a hundred or more years ago were frequently a medley of plants, such as hawthorn, privet and *Viburnum opulus,* the Guelder Rose. Today, they are usually formed of a single species. Here are a few to consider:

Fagus sylvatica (Common Beech): deciduous, with bright-green leaves in spring, darkening in summer and assuming rich tints in autumn; height 3–4 m; width 1–1.5 m; plant 45–60 cm apart.

Ligustrum ovalifolium (Privet or California Privet): evergreen or semi--evergreen (depending on the climate), with glossy, mid-green leaves; height 1.2–2 m; width 60–75 cm; plant 30–35 cm apart

Taxus baccata (Yew): evergreen conifer with narrow, dark-green leaves; ideal for creating arches or topiary; height 2–2.5 m; width 75–90 cm; plant 45 cm apart.

Internal hedges Many relatively low-growing and flowering shrubs can be used:

Fuchsia magellanica 'Riccartonii': tender, deciduous shrub with red and purple flowers from midsummer to the autumn; lax appearance, and ideal in coastal areas; height 1.1–1.2 m; width 60–90 cm; plant approximately 30–35 cm apart.

Lavandula angustifolia (also known as *L. spica* and *L. officinalis* – lavender): evergreen shrub with aromatic foliage and pale, grey-blue flowers from mid- to late summer; ideal for planting either side of a path; height 75–90 cm; width 45–60 cm; plant approximately 35–45 cm apart

Potentilla fruticosa (Shrubby Cinque-foil, Golden Hardhack and Widdy): hardy, deciduous shrub with pale-green leaves and buttercup-yellow flowers from late spring into much of summer; height 1.4–1.5 m; width 60 cm; plant about 25–30 cm apart.

THE HEALING INFLUENCE OF FENCES AND WALLS

It might sound strange that the size and nature of fences and walls can influence our lives, but anyone who has been confined to a small area will confirm that it is not conducive to health and happiness.

Fences

The range of fences is wide and not confined to bland screens of wood, although even those with a drab appearance can be made visually stimulating by a coating of preservative. High fences create privacy, but may make a garden appear claustrophobic. Therefore, keep fences as low as practicable.

Closeboard and panel fencing offers the most privacy, and is usually chosen for back gardens. Front gardens, however, need something lower and more decorative.

Right While picket fencing creates on attractive cottage-garden setting to borders, especially those formed of a medley of border plants with flowers that reveal differing shapes and colours.

Ranch-style fencing painted white and about 1 m high creates a clinical perimeter, ideal for modern houses. Because the planks of wood are horizontal, they do not confuse the eye, and they allow clear vision over it and into the distance.

White picket fencing, however, captures more attention and tends to confuse and distract the eye from immediately looking beyond the fence. Generally speaking, picket fencing is best suited to older properties, perhaps of a Colonial style.

Post and chain fencing, with vertical posts (often painted white) 30–45 cm high and about 1.5 m apart with an ornamental chain strung between them, is solely for marking a boundary. It does not form a barricade.

Walls

A high wall, perhaps rising to 2 m or more and constructed without any

Left: Hedges and statues are a useful combination in directing and focusing attention in gardens and to areas beyond. The gap in the hedge leads the eye to the statue, which should not dominate the hedge.

thought of introducing a decorative pattern into the brickwork, can be really depressing; the sooner it is clothed in wall shrubs or climbers, the better.

Walls are expensive to construct initially but are long-lasting, and with the wide range of brick materials now readily available, they can be given a decorative appearance.

Reconstituted stone blocks in varying sizes and shapes create attractive walls; lattice-like screen-brick walling blocks can be incorporated in them to produce a more decorative feature.

LABYRINTHS AND MAZES

Greeks and Romans knew buildings that were partly or wholly underground as 'labyrinths'; they had intricate passages and many chambers. During the Middle Ages, from the fifth century AD to about 1500, mazes (sometimes called labyrinths) were often drawn on the floors of French cathedrals. They were also marked on pavements or cut into turf outside churches, so that penitents could follow the lines on their knees – a symbolic journey for those who failed to undertake a pilgrimage to Jerusalem.

Mazes became part of European gardens in the sixteenth and seventeenth centuries. At first

they were formed of low shrubs and resembled knot gardens. The use of hedges appears to be a late seventeenth-century development, often forming complex patterns with several entrances. The famous maze at Hampton Court dates from about 1690, while in the 1700s the Governor's Palace at Williamsburg, capital of Virginia, had a maze with hedges formed of American Holly.

Many hedging plants have been used, including yew (*Taxus baccata*), holly (*Ilex aquifolium*), hornbeam (*Carpinus betulus*), and beech (*Fagus sylvatica*).

Free-standing trelliswork This offers the opportunity to form screens of climbing plants within a garden, or when positioned 60–75 cm from a boundary, to add extra privacy to both front and back gardens.

THE ART OF TOPIARY

Topiary is the art of shaping shrubs and trees by training and clipping them regularly. It is a skill that has been pursued for at least 2000 years; the Roman naturalist Pliny the Elder (AD 23–79) wrote of hunting scenes and ships clipped out of cypress, while clipped box (*Buxus sempervirens*) was often used to spell the name of the master of the garden and house.

The Romans first introduced the techniques of topiary to Britain and northern Europe and applied them to the gardens of their villas. When the Romans left Britain, it was mainly monasteries that kept the art alive, and it was not until Tudor and Elizabethan times that topiary again became a widely known craft in Britain, as well as mainland Europe.

In Florence, spheres, porticoes, temples, urns, donkeys, apes and bears were formed out of clipped evergreens. In Britain during the 1600s, plants such as thrift, hyssop, lavender, germander and thyme were widely used. Passion for the art continued until the eighteenth century, with figures clipped in box, rosemary and juniper. At that time, topiary was mainly pursued in large, stately gardens, but slowly it became part of many country gardens, with a resurgence of interest in the nineteenth century.

The positioning of topiary is very important, and whereas in cottage gardens images of animals can be placed to amuse, perhaps peering out of the medley of border plants, in open and more formal areas, where the topiary might form a focal point, it needs siting so that it readily captures attention.

Formal areas can be fringed with topiary formed into spheres, cones, squares or a variety of other figures.

Above right Clipped box hedges and topiary form a pleasing partnership with the white picket fencing. Shaped finials give the fencing added interest.

Many different plants have been used to create topiary, and in North America *Buxus sempervirens* (Common Box), cupressus, juniperus, *Ligustrum ovalifolium* (privet), *Taxus baccata* (yew), tsuga and *Eugenia uniflora* (Surinam Cherry, Brazil Cherry, Pitanga) have been used.

Creating a topiary figure is a long-term project, and one that could take several years before an identifiable image is created. In addition to pinching out shoot tips and clipping regularly, wire frameworks are essential to create the basic outline and to give support. Once established regular clipping is essential.

PONDS AND FOUNTAINS

Designing a garden feature so that its shape does not confuse the eye – and thereby cause mental aberration – is important. Like many other garden features, the perception of a pond's shape can dramatically change depending on the position from where it is viewed. A perfectly round pond when seen from a distance becomes oval; however, if viewed from a high terrace or on upper-floor window, it may resume much of its round outline.

Square ponds look fine when seen from relatively close by, but when viewed from a distance, and especially from a position that is raised, can be confusing to the eye. Rectangular ponds, with their longer lateral lines in proportion to the ends, do not usually suffer from this problem.

The perception of the height and shape of a cascade formed by a fountain may change depending on whether the outline if the spray is seen from the same level and close by, or from an elevated position some distance away. Try to position so that the upper third of the cascade – when viewed from on elevated distance – can be clearly seen above the pond's edge. If not, the fountain will merge with the pond, and its impact will be lost.

Left: An informal pond with the addition of a bridge creates on attractive feature. The natural slope of the land, together with trees and flowering shrubs, frame the pond, as well as directing attention to the white building, which from this angle is visually balanced by the white bridge.

HEALING SCENTS

Scent is the unseen power that strongly influences lives, from infancy onwards.
Babies detect their mother's milk partly through smell, while important
happenings in our lives are often recalled through distinctive scents: many people
remember the fragrance of their wedding bouquet for ever.

Our interest in scents is not surprising. During the mid-twentieth century, Dr Louis Leakey, the world-renowned Kenya-born anthropologist, suggested than Man survived his early years on earth because of his distinctive body odour, which was so offensive that it repelled predators! Dr Leakey speculated that Man's repulsive odour only began to disappear when he developed weapons for protection.

Scents, whether to repel or attract, have long been part of our lives, and it is not surprising that large financial resources are spent annually either to cloak body aromas or to create others with exciting, mate-attracting qualities. Similarly, many plants lure pollinating insects by having scented flowers – some sweet and alluring, but others putrid and offensive, like rancid meat, and ideal for enticing flies and bluebottles. However, scents are not solely present to help perpetuate the species: those in leaves provide some plants with protection against

insects such as ants, while in others they are an alternative to thorns in creating a defence against animals. Also, as most highly aromatic plants grow in hot and often dry regions, the aromatic oils form an oily vapour barrier that protects them from desiccation. In some plants, these oils also help to keep them free from fungal infestations and bacteria.

An additional role of scent in plants is as an antiseptic curative. The Balsam Fir, *Abies balsamea,* native to North America, produces an antiseptic, gumlike substance that solidifies when wounds are made in the bark. It was also

employed by early Man to treat his own health problems: the gum has a distinctive aroma and is ideal in the treatment of catarrh and in poultices.

Such are the antiseptic qualities of some plants that sprigs of both rue and rosemary were previously worn by judges and jurors in courts as a preventative against gaol fever.

Many plants with fragrant foliage, such as rosemary, thyme and lavender, are said to 'cool' the air. Earlier, these plants, along with basil, bee balm, camomile, costmary, hyssop and sage, were strewn in churches, castles and other buildings to create a pleasant aroma and cooling ambience.

The Scented Rush, *Acorus calamus* (sometimes known as the Sweet Sedge, Sweet Flag, Sweet Rush and Flagroot), was widely used for strewing in buildings in the sixteenth century; when strewn and crushed it gave off a fresh, fruity, cinnamon and somewhat tangerine-like bouquet.

Facing page: Cottage-style gardens, with their relaxed nature, create a wonderful range of healing scents throughout summer. Hedges help to reduce the strength of winds which disperse fragrance.

Above left: Lavender, like many garden plants, can be cut and dried during summer to produce fragrance indoors in winter.

THE HEALING AND COMFORTING QUALITIES OF SCENT

The creation of a restful yet stimulating environment, full of interesting fragrances, encourages the healing process. Minds relax, but are also kept active and responsive by the wide range of fragrances that plants create in gardens.

Many of the essential oils used in aromatherapy are perfect for creating interesting aromas indoors.

Some fragrances, such as honey, resin and musk, are wam and reassuring, while others with fruit-like redolences resembling raspberries, apples and pineapples are the epitome of summer and slightly more stimulating.

Personal choices

Most people have strong preferences about the scents they find appealing. However, the comforting powers of scents are not always a result of the

pleasantness of the smell, but because the fragrance is evocative and engenders memories of earlier times. Marriage services can be recalled through the sweetness of a bouquet of flowers: later, this often encourages the planting of a particular plant, shrub or tree.

For some people, certain fragrances are reminiscent of honeymoon locations; perhaps Hawaii, with the heavy scents of lush foliage and the sweet smell of tropical flowers like plumella, or Canada, with the resinous scent of pine trees. Even the scent given off by a wet dog after a winter's walk is evocative of an earlier age and, perhaps, a treasured pet.

The Curry Plant, *Helichrysum italicum* (still better known by its early name, H. *angustifolium)*, smells remarkably like curry powder, conjuring memories of savoury curry dishes.

Clearly, any scent that engenders memories of happy times has a healing nature. Conversely, aromas from not so memorable school days – perhaps cafeterias smelling of cabbage brewed for at least four hours, or sweat-drenched locker rooms marshalled by latter-day relations of Genghis Khan – may jar the memory, but certainly will not be comforting.

SAURUROS

*The North American Swamp Lizard (*Saururus cernuus) *grows in moist soil at the edges of ponds and develops slightly fragrant white flowers during summer. Native Americans boiled the roots to make a potion to heal flesh wounds.*

CATS' DELIGHT!

Above centre: Several diminutive spring-flowering bulbs bring colour and fragrance to rock gardens and path edges. The Snowdrop, *Galanthus elwesii* (in the foreground of the picture), is violet scented, while the Spring Snowflake, *Leucojum vernum* (top of picture), has sweetly scented flowers.

Right Catmint *Nepeta × faassenii,* has a similar bouquet to *Nepeta cataria* and is frequently planted alongside paths.

Nepeta or kattesminte, *Nepeta cataria* (now known as catnip or catnep) was grown in English gardens as early as 1263. Native to Europe and Asia, and now widely grown in North America, it is an irresistible attraction to some cats, which cannot resist rolling in the pungent foliage. Joseph Tournefort, the seventeenth-century French botanist, wrote that cats are aware of it, even when hidden.

Strangely, cats are more likely to destroy transplanted plants than seedlings, encouraging the saying:

If you set it, the cats will get it,
If you sow it, the cats won't know it.

Nicholas Culpeper, the seventeenth-century herbalist, recommended a tea infused from the leaves to control fevers and to encourage sleep.

For some men, romantic interludes with earlier girlfriends can be recalled through scents: redheads are said to smell of violets, brunettes to exude a musky redolence, while blondes are claimed to have the bouquet of ambergris. Conversely, one of the mistresses of the world-famous English writer H. G. Wells is said to have been comforted by the sweet, rich bouquet of honey which his body exuded.

Sweaty bodies do not usually encourage memories of happy times, but Napoleon, at the height of his romance with Josephine, would send home orders requesting her not to wash, as he would be with her within a few days. He might have been in the minority with his preference for perspiration, but like many other people he found the subtle fragrance of violets appealing and memorable. He derived pleasure and comfort from violets, and gave bouquets of them to Josephine on their wedding anniversaries; when banished to Elba, he said: 'I will return with the violets in the spring.' For this reason, violets became a symbol of Bonapartists, and he became known as 'Père Violette'. After his defeat at Waterloo and before his departure to St Helena, he is said to have visited Josephine's grave, where he picked violets, their favourite flower, which he carefully placed in a locket.

Soul-comforting incense

Scent imprinting was an early part of some religions, creating an atmosphere of rest and spiritual awareness. The Egyptians believed cedar wood to be imperishable and able to preserve any one enclosed in it, and cedar oil was rubbed into bodies and the wood burnt as incense, an offering to the gods. Egyptians believed their prayers, when mixed with incense smoke, would more rapidly ascend to heaven.

The Koran, the Holy Scripture for Muslims and a supreme classic of Arabic literature, describes Paradise as being filled with nymphs created out of musk. Indeed, the followers of the Prophet

Left: Pink Jasmine, *Jasminum polyanthum*, a slightly tender semi evergreen climber, has sweetly scented flowers that smother rustic arches and latticework secured to sheltered walls.

Muhammad were so fond of musk that it was frequently mixed with mortar in the construction of temples. The lasting scent of these buildings brings comfort to the followers of Muhammad.

In China, about 500 BC, the now world-renowned philosopher Confucius wrote that temples were hung with blossoms of magnolia, peach, jasmine and jonquil. Incense was burned in homes as well as temples.

Burning incense was adopted by the Christian faith, and became part of many religious services.

Fresh air

One person's fresh air is, of course, another's draught, but an abundance of fresh mountain air was recommended for

illnesses such as tuberculosis and anaemia; at lower altitudes, clean air when combined with the bouquet of pine trees was said to be ideal for convalescence. This also applied to coastal areas, where the fresh, bracing, sea was often combined with the redolence of pine trees.

The distinctive and cleansing smell of creosote, with its ability to revive memories of blocks of carbolic soap, has be used in the treatment of pulmonary tuberculosis; it was administered either suspended in a mucilage or in capsules. In addition, because of its local antiseptic and anaesthetic action, wood-tar creosote was used to relieve gastric pain due to ulcers when inhaled, it brought relief to sufferers bronchitis and other lung problems.

REPELLING INSECTS AND MICE

Several essential oils help to repel insects. Mosquitoes, for example, can be kept at bay by a few drops of citronella oil on clothing; when placed on pillowcases, it keeps them away at night. Most insects, including fleas and ants, are deterred by a mixture of thyme and Tea Tree, while the flying types are discouraged by lemongrass: mix it with water, place in a pump-action spray bottle, and mist the air when insects appear. Dog and cat fleas can be thwarted by a mixture of geranium and lavender. Spray into brushed fur, but make sure that it does not get into the pet's eyes. Mice can be very troublesome, but are known to keep away from areas liberally sprinkled with peppermint.

Above centre: Angelica (*Angelica archangelica*), a perennial often grown as a biennial, has seeds with a musk like scent.

SOURCES OF ESSENTIAL OILS

Because aromatherapists usually only use the common names of essential oils, botanical ones often become neglected. Therefore, a wide range of aromatherapy oils, together with the botanical names of the plants that provide them, are given here:

Angelico – *Angelica archangelica* (above)
Balm – *Melissa officinalis*
Basil – *Ocimum basilicum*
Bergamot – *Citrus bergamia*
Black Pepper – *Piper nigrum*
Calendula (Marigold) – *Calendula officinalis*
Camomile – *Matricaria recutita*
Camphor – *Cinnamomum camphora*
Cedar wood – *Cedrus atlantica*
Citronella – *Cymbopogon nardus*

Clary Sage – *Salvia sclarea*
Clove – *Syzygium aromaticum*
Cypress – *Cupressus sempervirens*
Eucalyptus – *Eucalyptus globules*
Fennel – *Foeniculum vulgare*
Geranium – *Pelargonium graveolens*
Ginger – *Zingiber officinale*
Jasmine – *Jasminum officinale*
Juniper – *Juniperus communis*
Laurel – *Laurus nobilis*
Lavender – *Lavandula angustifolio*
Lemon – *Citrus limon*
Lemongrass – *Cymbopogon citratus*
Lime – *Citrus aurantifolia*
Mandarin – *Citrus reticulata*
Marjoram – *Origanum marjorana*

Mimosa – *Acacia dealbata*
Orange – *Citrus sinensis*
Pennyroyal – *Mentha pulegium*
Peppermint – *Mentha × piperita*
Rose – *Rosa damascena / Rosa centifolia*
Rosemary – *Rosmarinus officinalis*
Sage – *Salvia officinalis*
Sandalwood – *Santalum album*
Spruce – *Tsuga canadensis*
Sweet Flag – *Acorus calamus*
Tarragon – *Artemisia dracunculus*
Thyme – *Thymus vulgaris*
Valerian – *Valeriana officinalis*
Violet – *Viola odorata*
Yarrow – *Achillea millefolium*
Ylang-ylang – *Canango odorata*

AROMATHERAPY – HOW IT BEGAN

The ancient Egyptians were among the earliest people to show an interest in perfumes. They involved them in religious rites, their toilet preparations, and body massages to increase the elasticity of skin, which is essential in hot climates, where it soon becomes dry and wrinkled.

The Egyptians were masters of perfumery, and began to import aromatic plants and potions 2000 years before the birth of Christ. The Greeks and Romans took up the use of oils; Julius Caesar (102–44 BC) forbade their use as he believed them to be effeminate, but Caligula (AD 12–41), a Roman Emperor, embraced them with enthusiasm. About 2000 years ago, the ever-spreading Roman Empire popularized the use of essential oils; later, Crusaders returning to Europe from the Holy Land in the eleventh, twelfth and thirteenth centuries added to this knowledge.

During the sixteenth and seventeenth centuries, botanists classified plants according to their healing powers; by the early part of the 1700s, thirteen essential oils had been listed for use in medicine. Slowly, however, science took pride of place, and research into plants as herbal cures diminished.

Then, in the early part of the 1900s, chance played an important role: the French chemist Gattefossé accidentally discovered that lavender oil aided the healing of his burned hand. He was so impressed by the curative nature of the oil that he began a lifelong interest in the oils

SAFETY FIRST WITH ESSENTIAL OILS

Essential oils bring great pleasure, influencing moods and behaviour as well as improving our bodies, but care is needed when using them:

Never take essential oils internally.

Always measure out essential oils carefully, using no more than recommended. Some oils are toxic when used in large amounts.

Do not apply them in an undiluted form to the skin; dilute them in carrier such as oil or water. Add them to water for use in inhalations, baths and room sprays, and to a carrier oil for massages, as well as body moisturizers for beauty treatments.

Keep essential oils in airtight, dark glass bottles in cool places out of direct sunlight. Never put them in plastic containers, or they could become contaminated.

After using oils on the body, allow 24 hours for them to penetrate the skin before taking a bath or shower.

If an essential oil splashes into an eye, rinse it with a few drops of Sweet Almond oil – do not use water – and consult a doctor immediately.

Some oils should not be used during pregnancy, and these include angelica, basil, fennel, juniper, laurel, marjoram, rosemary, tarragon, thyme and yarrow. While pregnant, always consult a doctor before using any medications or essential oils!

A few essential oils cause skin irritation, especially if exposed to sunshine soon after application. The remedy is either to stay indoors for about eight hours after use, or to use the oil at half, or less, the recommended strength.

Oils that can cause irritation include angelica, bergamot, citronella, lemon, lime and orange.

Consult a doctor if irritation occurs.

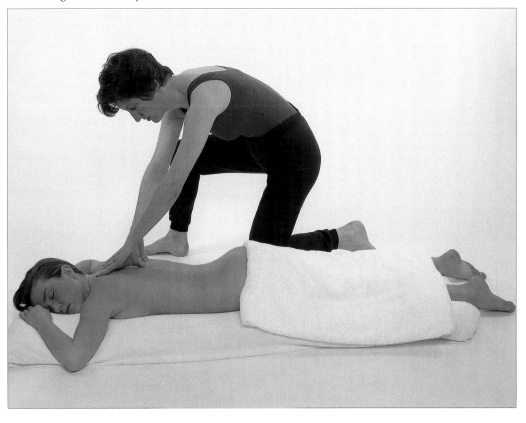

of plants, and it was he who coined the term 'aromatherapy', and in 1928 wrote the first book on this subject.

Goddissart, another Frenchman, who was working in Los Angeles in 1938, reported that essential oils were excellent in the treatment of skin cancer and in healing wounds.

Essential oils

Volatile oils have the characteristic odour of the plant they come from. They are employed to make perfumes and lotions, as well as flavourings. These oils are held in minute sacs on the plants, and are usually taken from leaves and petals, although they also occur in roots, stems, sap, bark and seeds. For example, with rosemary the leaves are used, with lavender the flowers, with sandalwood the bark, with Sweet Flag the roots, and with myrrh the resin.

These essential oils must be used in a pure form, and for that reason are best bought from reputable shops.

TOPICAL TANSY

For many centuries tansy,
Tanaceturn vulgare *(also known as Golden Buttons), has been popular, and it is said to have been used by ancient Greeks to preserve bodies from corruption. In Renaissance palaces it became part of stillrooms where ladies could amuse themselves distilling scents, while in the fifteenth and sixteenth centuries it was used as a strewing herb; it was said to keep away flies, and to be especially effective when mixed with elder leaves.*

Right: Rosemary, thyme *(top center)*, camomile *(far right)* and fennel *(facing page)* all supply essential oils.

Using aromatherapy oils

The oils are usually used to massage the body, but they are also vital constituents of beauty treatments or added to baths as a restorative.

Essential oils are present in plants in very small amounts – it takes about 900 Kg of rose petals to produce 450 g of rose oil.

There are two distinct methods of extracting oil from leaves, stems and other parts of plants: distillation and enfleurage.

Distillation uses heat – and, later, condensation – to separate the oils. The oils produced by this method are not as prized as those gained by enfleurage, which involves placing the plant material on filters positioned in a bowl of oil. Slowly, the oil absorbs the essential oils in the plants. As plants become exhausted of oils, it is necessary to replace them with fresh material, a process that continues until the oil in the bowl is completely saturated. The essence is extracted from the oil by distillation, and then dissolved in vegetable oils.

AROMATHERAPY – RANGE OF OILS

The range of essential oils is wide, and at first glance appears bewildering, but most have familiar common names, and many come from plants widely seen in gardens.

Using essential oils

These are used to treat many medicinal problems:

Acne: bergamot, cedarwood, geranium, juniper, sandalwood

Anxiety: bergamot, Clary Sage, lavender, mimosa, neroli, patchouli, sandalwood, violet

Athlete's foot: birch, geranium, lavender, lemongrass, Tea Tree

Backache: bay, camphor, citronella, Clary Sage, eucalyptus, lavender, pine, spruce

Bites and stings: basil, calendula (marigold), camomile, citronella, lavender, peppermint

Bruises: calendula (marigold), camphor, Clary Sage, geranium, marjoram

Burns: camomile, camphor, eucalyptus, geranium, lavender, rosemary

Chilblains: eucalyptus, ginger, juniper, lemon, marjoram, rosemary

Colds: basil, black pepper, camomile, camphor, eucalyptus, marjoram, peppermint, rosemary

Cramp: eucalyptus, lemon, marjoram

Fatigue: ambrette seeds, Clary Sage, eucalyptus, ginger, lavender, lemongrass, peppermint, rosemary, thyme

Hangover: geranium, lavender, neroli

Headache: eucalyptus, lavender, lemongrass, peppermint, violet

Indigestion: angelica, fennel, lavender, marjoram: peppermint

Insomnia: basil, camomile, cypress, geranium, lavender, mimosa, neroli, petitgrain, rose, ylang-ylang

Nausea: basil, lavender, lemon, peppermint, rosemary, thyme

Perspiration: bergamot, citronella, lemongrass, lavender, thyme

Poor circulation: basil, cedar wood, cypress, ginger, juniper, lavender, lemon, lemon-grass, pine, rosemary

Shock: camphor, orange blossom, peppermint

Stress: basil, bergamot, Clary Sage, geranium, jasmine, mandarin, marjoram, neroli, rose, sandalwood

Sunburn: camomile, geranium, lavender

Toothache: camphor, camomile, clove, pennyroyal, peppermint, sage

SAGEBRUSH MEDICINE

Also commonly known as Basin Sagebrush, Seriphidium tridentatum *(earlier and still better known as* Artemisa tridentata*) is native to North America, from California to British Columbia. It grows up to 3 m high, and at one time provided fuel, food and medicine for Native Americans, as well as early settlers. Stems and dried leaves were used as fuel for fires, the oily seeds were both chewed and employed to make flour, the leaves were used to ease stomach gas, while an infusion of leaves was used to ease headaches and colds.*

Left: An 'alchemist's' herb garden, given added interest and an aura of mystique by jars which could have come from an old apothecary. Take care that glass containers are not exposed to boisterous children or animals.

CARDAMOM

*Cardamom (Elettaria
Cardamom) native to southern
India, has seeds that yield an
aphrodisiac essential oil. Also
known as Malabar and Ceylon
Cardamom, the seeds were
mentioned in a Kama Sutra
recipe, suggesting it should be
mixed with ginger and
cinnamon and spread over peas
and onions. In addition, whole
cardamom seeds are used to
flavor curries and marinades.*

Right: The New English
Rose 'Constance Spry' has a
strong fragrance of myrrh.
It was introduced in the
early 1960s, develops
magnificent clear pink
blooms and can be grown
as a shrub or climber.

Facing page: The Gallica Rose
'Charles de Mille' has
moderately scented, rich
crimson flowers that assume
tints of purple as they age.

DETECTING SCENTS AND HEALING FRAGRANCES

The rich parade of scents in gardens creates healing balms that enrich our lives, either through their medical powers or just for interest and amusement. However, we do not all detect smells to the same degree; women have a greater ability to appreciate smells than men, but while pregnant this power decreases. In addition, dark-haired people have a more alert sense of smell than those who are fair-haired, while albinos have great difficulty in detecting aromas.

Sinus problems temporarily reduce the ability to detect smells, while people working indoors are usually better able to detect and identify aromas than those employed outdoors.

Regardless of lifestyle, people are sensitive to different scents. A rose may smell sweet to one person and have little or no scent to another.

CLASSIFYING SCENTS

Arranging the scents of flowers, leaves, roots, wood and bark into logical

groupings is not easy; an attempt was made at the end of the 1800s, placing them in six groups, later enlarged to ten.

More than 100 different scents can be featured in gardens. Some of these have a comforting nature, while others are more likely to make noses twitch, and include fishy overtones and the fetid nature of decaying flesh.

The range of exciting scents is wide, and they seldom fail to amuse, stimulate, soothe and revitalize the mind.

Redolence in flowers

Flowers with a fetid nature have the distinctive aroma of decaying meat and fish, and include the well-known North American plants Skunk Cabbage (*Lysichiton americanus*) and Squawroot or Stinking Benjamin (*Trillium erectum*).

Fishy odours, resembling ammonia, are unforgettable and often suggest stale perspiration. Plants offering these smells include trees and shrubs in the hawthorn, cotoneaster and amelanchier families.

Sweet and heavy fragrances are much more comforting and pleasing, and are frequently sought in gardens. Plants to create these redolences include the

TASMANIAN BLUE GUM

Also known as time Fever Tree, the Australian tree Eucalyptus globulus bears leaves with a bitter, pungent, camphoric taste and smell. They yield a volatile oil earlier used by Aborigines as a remedy for fevers, to ease muscular aches, and to heal wounds. The oil contains eucalyptol and is used in baths, inhalations and massages. An antiseptic, it kills airborne germs. Indeed, in the 1800s the tree was introduced to Italy and planted in malarial districts.

CLEANING AND PURIFYING THE HOME

Many essential oils are ideal as household cleansers and air purifiers, as they create superb fragrances that cloak bad smells and enrich the air with aromas that soothe tiredness and irritability.

To clean surfaces, add a few drops of the oils to a bowl of warm water, soak a cloth in it and then wring out. Oils to use to scent and clean surfaces in kitchens are lemon and geranium; for including in

washing-up water try geranium and lavender; for toilets pine and Tea Tree are ideal, and for baths and sinks use lavender and lemon.

To add vitality to air, put a few drops of the oils on a cotton-wool ball and place it inside your vacuum cleaner. Some of the best essential oils for purifying homes are bergamot, citronella, lemon, peppermint, pine, rosemary and Tea Tree.

times the hedge's height the reduction is only 20 per cent.

Hedges are better than walls and fences at creating microclimates for plants. When wind comes up against a wall, it produces turbulence on both the lee and windward sides, whereas a hedge filters the wind without creating damaging eddies.

When planting a hedge, plan carefully so it does not create a frost pocket. Frost-saturated air naturally travels downhill and often just passes over plants, causing little damage. However, when the passage of frost is blocked it builds up to the height of the hedge and then spills over the top. The cold, frost-laden area can be especially damaging to spring-flowering shrubs and fruit trees when in blossom.

Deciduous hedges, of course, are less restrictive than evergreen types, but both reduce the flow of air.

Fragrant conifers

Many hardy and tough hedging conifers have foliage that when stroked and crushed reveal distinctive and attractive bouquets; these include the redolence of resin and parsley (Lawson False Cypress – *Chamaecyparis lawsoniana*), fruity and resembling apples (White Cedar – *Thuja occidentalis*), lemon (Monterey Cypress – *Cupressus macrocarpa*), and pineapple (Western Red Cedar – *Thuja plicata*). Furthermore, several of these conifers have forms with attractively coloured foliage, helping to create a colourful as well as scented boundary.

When planting a boundary hedge, always position the trunks at least half the expected width of hedge in from the boundary line. Foliage that trespasses into a neighbour's garden eventually becomes a nuisance and, sometimes, a matter of serious legal dispute.

Coastal hedges

Winds sweeping in off the sea create problems of wind-buffeting damage, as well as the risk of foliage being seared by salt-laden gusts. Several conifers with fragrant foliage are resistant to coastal damage, and these include the North American Monterey Cypress, *Cupressus*

Right: All scented gardens benefit from carefully positioned seats which allow the fragrance of flowers to be appreciated in a relaxed way during summer evenings. This unusual and canopied garden bench has handles so it easily can be moved indoors during winter.

macrocarpa. The normal form has bright-green leaves in densely packed sprays, but for extra colour try the variety 'Goldcrest' with feathery, rich-yellow juvenile foliage.

Some fragrant shrubs are sufficiently hardy for coastal areas, and those suitable for planting as hedges – or just to create shelter for other plants – include the Double-flowered Gorse, *Ulex europaeus* 'Flore Plena' (also known as whin or furze). During late spring and early summer – and sometimes intermittently until winter – it bears chrome-yellow, honey-scented, double flowers amid spiny, branched stems.

The Daisy Bush, *Olearia × haastii*, an evergreen shrub, grows up to about 2.5 m high, and has white-felted dark green leaves and heads of white, fragrant flowers during midsummer.

Low-growing hedges

Within gardens, smaller hedging plants with both fragrant flowers and foliage can be used to create extra shelter and to divide gardens. These shrubs range from lavender to rosemary, as well as scented climbers trailing over lattices. There is also the possibility of scented climbers such as the Mountain Clematis, *Clematis montana,* trailing over existing, and perhaps bare and unsightly, deciduous hedges.

Wind tunnels

These are created by the close proximity of houses and other buildings, which channel cold blasts into a garden. Planting tough conifers at corners helps to reduce the blast, but take care not to plant them too close to buildings, as several years later, when 4 m or more tall, they may cause subsidence to buildings and result in litigation with neighbours.

Lattices also help to diminish the wind's force, and although it may, at first, be difficult to establish climbing plants in such positions, most eventually survive. When these plants are young, form a screen 1–1.2 m high of straw sandwiched between two layers of plastic-mesh netting. Carefully form it into a U-shaped screen, and secure it in position with bamboo canes on the windward side of the plant.

EVENING- AND NIGHT-SCENTED GARDENS

In sixteenth century India, the bride of the mogul emperor Akbar introduced the idea of gardens planted for night-time pleasure. She used elements such as dark tree forms and pagodas outlined against the sky, contrasted with white scented blooms to reflect the moonlight.

Healing value of evening scents

The evening of each day is an important part of our lives – a time of rest, contemplation and preparation for the following day. In cooler regions, from autumn to late spring, evenings are usually passed indoors, perhaps listening to music, reading or watching television, but summer

Below: French Lavender, *Lavandula stoechas,* forms an evergreen shrub about 60 cm high, and is admirable for cloaking the side of a garden bench, where its fragrance can be readily appreciated.

evenings encourage relaxation on patios and terraces. Evenings may be passed sitting indoors near an open window, enjoying the stillness, colour and fragrance that scented gardens have to offer.

There is a wide range of evening- and night-scented plants: some, such as the Night-scented Stock, Vesper Flower and the climber *Lonicera caprifolium,* are well known for their evening fragrance. Many day-scented flowers, such as *Lonicera periclymenum,* also continue their fragrance into evening. Similarly, the well-known Flowering Tobacco Plant (*Nicotiana alata*) is sweetly fragrant during the day and just as evident during evenings.

Scented patios and terraces

As well as the opportunity to fill window boxes, hanging baskets and tubs with fragrant plants, flowerbeds under windows are ideal places for growing hardy annuals; these are sown directly into the soil in which they will germinate, grow and flower. Most well-known of these is the duo of Virginia Stock (*Malcolmia maritima*) and the Night-scented Stock (*Matthiola longipetala,* but better known by its earlier name, *Matthiola bicornis*). These two hardy annuals make an ideal combination: the Night-scented Stock has a sprawling nature with dull-lilac flowers that reveal their heavy, sweet and penetrating scent at night, while the Virginia Stock flowers throughout the day and has a neater nature.

Wide range of evening scents

Most of the fragrances at night are sweet, although a few offer fruity or magnolia redolences. Those with a sweet bouquet include the Sand Verbena, *Abronia fragrans,* a half-hardy perennial with exceptionally sweet, pure-white flowers that open on summer afternoons. The Spurge Laurel, *Daphne laureola,* is a hardy, evergreen shrub with sweet, greenish-yellow flowers during late winter and early spring.

The Flowering Tobacco Plant or Jasmine Tobacco Plant, *Nicotiana alata* (better known by its earlier name, *N. affinis*), is a half-hardy annual with exceptionally sweet, tubular, white flowers from mid- to late summer. With a name like Evening Primrose, *Oenothera biennis* is certain to flower during evenings. It is a hardy biennial with sweet, pale-yellow flowers from early to late summer.

Variously known as Border Phlox, Summer Phlox and Fall Phlox, *Phlox paniculata* is a herbaceous perennial with very sweet flowers borne in dense heads from mid- to late summer. Mignonette, *Reseda odorata,* popularized by the Empress Josephine, is a hardy annual with alluringly sweet, yellow-white flowers from early summer to the autumn. Widely known as Common Soapwort, Fuller's Herb and Bouncing Bet, *Saponaria officinalis*

Above right: Oils derived from the seeds of the Evening Primrose (*Oenothera*) are used to help with hormonal problems. A syrup made from the flowers is said to be beneficial in whooping cough.

Right Clusters of plants in pots on patios and terraces benefit from the warmth reflected by walls. They also appreciate the shelter from cold winds. This cluster of pots is backed by sage and scented pelargoniums.

is a hardy perennial with sweet, pink flowers from mid- to late summer. The Night-flowering Catch-fly or Sticky Cockle, *Silene noctiflora,* is a hardy annual with richly sweet, white or pink flowers during summer. The Nottingham Catchfly or Dover Catchfly, *Silene nutans,* has a herbaceous, perennial nature with richly sweet, white or pink flowers from early to midsummer.

Hesperis matronalis, variously known as Vesper Flower, Damask Violet, Dame's Rocket and Sweet Rocket, is a short-lived, hardy perennial with a sweet and penetrating scent from white, purple or mauve flowers during early and mid-summer. *Mirabilis jalapa* is a tender perennial best grown as an annual, with trumpet-like flowers from mid- to late summer. With a magnolia-like redolence, *Oenothera caespitosa* is well worth growing; it is a herbaceous perennial with white flowers from early to late summer.

SCENTED WINTER GARDENS

There can be few garden features so spiritually uplifting and healing as a scented winter garden. At a time when gloom often pervades the very fabric of life, a walk among fragrant shrubs and trees is a tonic – and one that everyone can enjoy.

Firm paths and shelter from strong winds are essential, and make sure the area does not trap cold, frost-saturated air.

Position winter-scented shrubs and trees so that their branches are relatively close to a path's edge, but make sure they are not obstructing it. This way the redolence is readily apparent without people having to tread on wet soil.

Scented shrubs and trees

Several attractive shrubs and trees flower during winter, in a range of fragrances. One of the most memorable of these is the Lily-of-the-Valley bouquet revealed by *Mahonia japonica,* an evergreen shrub with lemon-yellow flowers from midwinter to mid-spring. For a spicy and heavy fragrance, Winter Sweet is worth considering. Known as *Chimonanthus praecox* (earlier known as *C. fragrans*), it is a bushy, deciduous shrub with cup-shaped and clawlike, ivory-coloured petals and purple centres during midwinter.

Many winter-flowering shrubs develop sweetly scented flowers, and these

Left: The deciduous shrub Winter Sweet, *Chimonanthus praecox,* develops spicy scented flowers on leafless branches during midwinter.

WINDOW BOX DELIGHT

In the early 1800s, window boxes in London became packed with Sweet Mignonette, Reseda odorata, *which wafted its sweet, ambrosial scent throughout the streets. The passion for this flower began in France when the Empress Josephine set the fashion of growing it as a pot plant; Napoleon is said to have collected seeds of it during his Egyptian campaign. Although this distinctive plant cannot be said to be an aphrodisiac, it is claimed that success and good fortune attends the lover who rolls three times in a bed of mignonette!*

Right: The late-winter and early-spring flowering *Iris reticulata* develops flowers with a violet-like fragrance. As well as creating a superb display along the edges of paths, it can be planted in window boxes and other containers.

include *Daphne odora,* a slightly tender, evergreen shrub with pale-purple flowers from midwinter to mid-spring. In cold areas it needs shelter from cold winds. *Daphne odora* 'Aureomarginata' is slightly hardier, with creamy white edges to its shiny, mid-green leaves.

Few winter-flowering shrubs or small trees are as well known as the Japanese Witch Hazel, *Hamamelis japonica,* deciduous and with yellow, sometimes tinged red, spider-like, slightly scented flowers during late winter and into spring. The related Chinese Witch Hazel, *Hamamelis mollis,* is another deciduous shrub or small tree, with sweetly scented, golden yellow, spider-like flowers in clusters during midwinter. The partially evergreen shrub *Lonicera fragrantissima* has creamy-white, penetratingly sweet flowers from midwinter to early spring. The related *Lonicera standishii* is a deciduous shrub with sweet, creamy-white flowers from early winter to early spring.

Several mahonias have sweetly scented flowers in winter. *Mahonia* 'Charity' is an evergreen shrub with deep-yellow flowers in tapering, cascading spires from early to late winter. *Mahonia lomariifolia is* also evergreen, with deep-yellow, penetratingly sweet flowers in tapering spires from midwinter to late spring.

The deciduous shrub *Viburnum × bodnantense* 'Dawn' has sweet, white flowers, which are flushed pink and rose-red when in bud, in clusters on bare stems from early to late winter. *Viburnum farreri* (better known by its earlier and perhaps more descriptive name *V. fragrans) is* another deciduous shrub, with white flowers, tinged pink when in bud, borne in clusters from early to late winter.

The deciduous shrub *Viburnum grandiflorum* has deep-pink, sweetly scented flowers, carmine when in bud, from midwinter to spring.

For a pungent bouquet, the Osark Witch Hazel, *Hamamelis vernalis*, is worth growing. It is a suckering, deciduous shrub with clusters of small, crimped, pale to tawny-yellow petals during mid- and late winter.

ANCIENT MEDICINE

The Burning Bush,
Dictamnus albus, *has a*
long history as a medicinal
plant, with its roots once
used to treat fevers as well as
hysteria. More recently,
powdered roots mixed with
peppermint have been used to
treat epilepsy, while it is
claimed an infusion of the
leaves will remedy
nervousness.

Scented miniature conifers
for winter fragrance on patios

These are invaluable for adding scent during winter, and many can be planted in tubs and other large containers, or planted at the edges of patios and terraces. Their foliage, when gently crushed, yields many exciting fragrances.

Juniperus communis 'Compressa' is a narrow, columnar form with grey-blue foliage that reveals an apple-like bouquet. It is ideal for planting in window boxes and small tubs.

For an apple-like and fruity bouquet, American Arborvitae, also known as Eastern White Cedar (*Thuja occidentalis* 'Danica') is worth growing. It is bun-shaped with bright-green foliage. Plant it in a tub. *Thuja occidentalis* 'Rheingold' has a similar fragrance. It has a rounded habit, with old-gold foliage in summer, rich copper in winter. Plant it in a tub.

Thuja plicata 'Stoneham Gold' has closely packed, golden-yellow foliage with a fruity bouquet, reminiscent of pineapples. Plant it in a tub.

Chamaecyparis pisifera 'Filifera Aurea' is usually domed, with gold-yellow foliage that reveals a resinous bouquet. Plant it in a large tub.

For a resinous and parsley bouquet, plant Lawson false cypress (*Chamaecyparis lawsoniana* 'Minima Aurea'). It is conical, with golden-yellow foliage.

Winter-fragrant bulbs

These are diminutive, and ideal for planting under deciduous trees and shrubs or at the edges of winter-flowering borders. Plant them in groups, rather than spreading a few bulbs over a large area.

The range of fragrances is wide, and includes two with a honey bouquet: *Crocus chrysanthus* displays globelike, rich golden-yellow flowers during late winter, while *Iris danfordiae* develops vivid lemon flowers, lightly blotched brown, during mid- and late winter.

For an earthy, mosslike redolence, plant the Common Snowdrop, *Galanthus nivalis*. It has nodding, six-petalled white flowers with green markings on the inner petals

Above left: Water lilies are an important element in garden ponds, and many are sweetly scented. There are varieties to suit all depths of ponds.

from midwinter to early spring. Plant in pots for convenience.

Iris histrioides has sweet-smelling, dark blue flowers with pale and spotted areas around an orange crest in midwinter.

A violet-like fragrance is always welcome, and this is provided by *Galanthus elwesii*, a snowdrop with white, six-petalled flowers with deep green markings on the inner petals during late winter and early spring. The Netted Iris, *Iris reticulata* also has a violet bouquet, with deep-purple-blue flowers with orange blazes on the falls during late winter and early spring.

SCENTED PONDS AND BOG GARDENS

Few areas in gardens have such a curative and calming influence as ponds.

Calm water has a reflective nature, and this creates a healing and mentally rejuvenating ambience. Therefore, when rich and varied fragrances are added to these oases of contentment, they also help stimulate recovery.

The range of scented aquatic and bog garden plants is wide, and fragrances as varied as vanilla, musk, cinnamon,

brandy, almond and camphor, as well as sweetness, can be introduced.

Aquatic plants

Water has a magical and mystical nature, revealing only its surface, and keeping its depths hidden. Most scented aquatic plants are above the water's surface, but some are submerged.

The Yellow Pond Lily or Spatterdock, *Nuphar lutea*, is a hardy, perennial water plant with bright-yellow, faintly brandy-scented flowers 5–7.5 cm wide during mid- and late summer. Once established it is a vigorous water plant, and must be given plenty of space. Indeed, it looks at its best in large and dominant groups.

For a minty, tangy bouquet, the Water

Above centre: The North American Skunk Cabbage, *Lysichiton americanus,* derives its common name from the unpleasant smell emitted by the large, sulphur-yellow spathes. It is ideal for planting in moist soil surrounding a pond, or in a bog garden.

Right: Garden ponds packed with scented plants need not be isolated in a lawn; instead, they can be integrated with herbaceous plants and shrubs. Large pebbles help to soften the edges of ponds and to unify them with the rest of the garden.

Mint, *Mentha aquatica* (also known as Marsh Mint and Wild Mint), has few rivals. It is a hardy perennial, and ideal for planting in shallow water or marshy positions. Its aromatic, purple stems and small, lancelike leaves bear lilac to purple flowers during summer. Its redolence is so strong that it may overpower other plants. Nevertheless, it creates a superbly fresh ambience.

Some water lilies have sweetly scented flowers, and these include several varieties of *Nymphaea odorata,* the Fragrant Water Lily. It is a hardy perennial with large, nearly round, green leaves that float on the water's surface.

The vanilla-scented flowers of the Cape Pondweed or Water Hawthorn (*Aponogeton distachyos*) rise approximately 10 cm above the water's surface, amid narrow, oval, light green leaves with maroon-brown markings. A perennial, it creates a wealth of flowers year after year.

Bog garden and marginal plants

Areas of moist soil around ponds may, at first glance, appear to be inhospitable, but they can soon become awash with scented plants. Some moisture-loving plants have excitingly scented flowers, while others only reveal their redolence when stems or leaves are bruised or crushed.

The Meadowsweet or Queen of the Meadow, *Filipendula ulmaria,* is a hardy, herbaceous perennial, 60–90 cm high, with almond-scented, creamy-white flowers throughout summer. For the quite different aroma of camphor, *Cotula*

coronopifolia (widely known as Button-Weed or Brass Buttons) is an annual about 23 cm high, and well worth growing. It produces button-like, white or yellow flowers during mid- and late summer.

For a medley of aromas such as cinnamon, tangerine and fruit, the Variegated Sweet Flag, *Acorus calamnus* 'Variegatus', has few rivals. It is a hardy, herbaceous perennial that thrives in shallow water as well as constantly boggy soil at a pond's edge. It grows 1 m high, with broad, stiffly erect, swordlike leaves striped with white. When crushed, all parts – including the roots – have this medley of bouquets.

The musklike angelica, *Angelica archangelica,* is a short-lived perennial, up to 2 m high and with 8 cm wide, umbrella-like heads of greenish-white or green flowers during mid- and late summer. The whole plant has a strong, musky bouquet.

The hardy, herbaceous perennial Swamp Lily, Water Dragon or Lizard's Tail, *Saururus cernuus,* is a herbaceous perennial for planting in moist soil at the edge of a pond or in water up to 5 cm deep. It develops white flowers amid green, heart-shaped leaves during mid summer. In contrast, and with a tangy aroma, *Houttuynia cordata* 'Plena' is a hardy, herbaceous perennial that is ideal for planting in wet soil or 2.5–5 cm of water. During summer it develops clustered heads of white flowers amid metallic, blue-green, heart-shaped leaves.

The beautiful Winter Heliotrope, *Petasites fragrans,* is a herbaceous perennial with roundish, toothed leaves, and lilac, vanilla-scented flowers; some people claim it is more reminiscent of almonds,

Above: Water lilies must be grown in individual containers, so initially they can be positioned on several bricks so the leaves are not submerged; as the leaf stalks grow, the bricks can be removed and the container lowered into the water.

SCENTED ROSE GARDENS

Rose gardens not steeped in exciting fragrances are like roast beef without Yorkshire pudding or strawberries without cream. However, some devotees of roses seem to have more enthusiasm for the shape and colour of the flowers than the wide range of fragrances these cherished shrubs can offer. These bouquets range from the fresh redolence of apples to the Oriental undertones of musk and the fruitlike bouquet of bananas.

These rich and varied fragrances are mostly found in two groups of roses: species roses and their natural and

CURING EYE DISEASES

The Asian Houttuynia cordata *has leaves used in the treatment of eye diseases, as well as for adding to salads. In China, the whole plant is used in the treatment of kidney amid bladder complaints and skin diseases.*

Right: Scented climbing roses festooning walls, pergolas and lattices are a memorable sight. Here is the New English Rose 'Heritage', which creates a mass of cupped, purest shell-pink flowers with an Old Rose fragrance and strong overtones of lemon. It flowers regularly throughout summer. Usually, this rose forms a small bush, but if given a warm, sheltered position it can be used to cloak a wall.

Facing page: The Gallica rose 'Tuscany Superb' creates a bush about 1.5 m high bearing deep crimson, fragrant flowers that fade to purple.

man-made crosses, and especially the 'Old Roses', which originated before 1867. Within the past thirty years or so, many richly scented roses have been created by David Austin and are now known as 'New English Roses'.

Fragrant roses have long been grown in our gardens, and planting a few of them markedly enhances a garden. (Scented climbing and rambling roses are featured on pages 88 and 89.)

Range of fragrances

Apple: 'Max Graf' has a shrubby nature, and is ideal as ground cover, where it reveals single, pink flowers with lighter centres. 'Nymphenburg' also presents this redolence in its fully double, warm salmon-pink flowers shaded cerise and with orange-yellow at the base of each petal.

Bananas: This unusual bouquet is revealed in 'Dupontii', a wild rose hybrid shrub with blush-white, cream-tinted flowers showing yellow anthers.

Clove: The cluster-flowered shrub 'Fritz Nobis' develops flesh-pink flowers with darker shadings. With a ground-covering nature, *Rosa paulii*, a hybrid of wild roses, has pure white flowers and golden stamens.

Fruity: Several New English Roses have this pleasing fragrance: 'Abraham Darby' reveals large, cupped blooms in shades of yellow and apricot; 'Charles Austin' develops cupped blooms in shades of apricot and yellow, and paling with age; while 'Belle Story' has with large, pale pink flowers and central bosses of stamens.

Lemon: There are several roses with this fresh and pleasant bouquet. 'Mme Hardy' is a Damask type with large, double, white blooms, initially cupped. The Hybrid Tea 'Blue Moon' has large, lilac-mauve blooms on upright, branching bushes, while the New English Rose 'Heritage' reveals medium-sized, cupped, shell-pink flowers.

Lilac: This is an early summer bouquet, which is very welcome in a rose. The

Modern Shrub Rose 'Lavender Lassie' reveals this fragrance in its medium-sized, double, pink blooms shaded with lavender.

Lily-of-the-Valley: This penetrating fragrance is to be found in 'Double White', which is derived from *Rosa pimpinellifolia*, the Scotch or Burnet Rose. It has small, fully double, white blooms.

Musk: This bouquet reminiscent of the East is to be found in several roses. 'Cardinal Hume' is a New English Rose with deep-purple flowers that reveal the shape and style of Old Roses, while 'Daybreak' is a Hybrid Musk with bunches of small, rich yellow buds that open to reveal semi-double, yellow flowers with dark gold stamens. 'Moonlight' is another Hybrid Musk, with semi-double, creamy-white flowers borne in very large trusses.

Myrrh: Several New English Roses reveal this redolence, including 'Chaucer' with deeply cupped, rose-pink flowers. Others are 'Cressida', which develops large, apricot-pink flowers, and

'Cymbeline' with large, loosely double, grey-pink flowers.

'Old Rose' fragrance: This bouquet is a rich medley of fragrances revealed by a couple of New English Roses, including 'Othello', with large, full-petalled, rich dusky crimson flowers which later turn to shades of mauve and purple. Another is 'The Countryman', the product of a New English Rose crossed with a Portland rose, with rose-pink flowers that open flat to reveal a many-petalled rosette.

Raspberry: Several roses have this fresh, fruity bouquet. 'Adam Messerich', a Bourbon Rose, has large, semidouble, rich pink flowers, while 'Honorine de Brabant', a Bourbon Rose, develops pale-pink flowers, striped and spotted with crimson and mauve. 'Cerise Bouquet' is another rose with this fragrance; a Modern Shrub Rose with large sprays of semidouble, cerise-pink flowers. *Rosa canina* 'Andersonii', a wild rose hybrid with brilliant pink, single flowers, also reveals a raspberry fragrance.

Sweet Pea: This is a unique fragrance, and one that is revealed by 'Vanity', a Hybrid Musk with large, single, deep-pink flowers borne in dainty sprays.

Tea Rose: This fragrance needs explanation, as it encompasses those flowers that smell of a freshly opened packet of tea. 'Buff Beauty', a Hybrid Musk with medium-sized, warm apricot-yellow blooms in large trusses, has this redolence, together with 'Graham Thomas', a New English Rose with medium-sized, cup-shaped, rich yellow

flowers. 'Lady Hillingdon', a Tea Rose, has beautiful buds and flowers in shades of pink, while 'Le Vesuve', a China Rose, develops creamy-pink buds opening to a beautiful coppery-pink.

SCENTED CLIMBERS

Few garden features are as attractive as scented climbers clothing lattices, arbours, pergolas and rustic poles. The range of scents is wide – some are heavy, sweet and soporific, especially during warm summer afternoons, while others are exciting through their unexpectedness, and range from myrrh to apple, clover and vanilla. Both roses and other climbers contribute to these redolences.

Fragrant climbers

Sweetness is the bouquet offered by most climbers, but others have more varied and exciting fragrances:

Cowslip: The deciduous *Clematis rehderiana* develops small, bell-shaped and nodding, greenish-yellow flowers during late summer and autumn.

Hawthorn: The Fragrant Virgin's Bower, *Clematis flammula*, is a deciduous climber that bears shining white flowers in lax groups during late summer and into autumn.

Honey: This somewhat heady redolence is revealed by *Lonicera × americana*, a semi evergreen or deciduous climber with white or cream flowers becoming yellow and tinged purple on the outside during midsummer. A related species, *Lonicera × heckrottii*, is hardy, deciduous

APOTHECARY'S ROSE

During the thirteenth century, the town of Provins, south-east of Paris, became famous for an industry that lasted at least 600 years. A red, semi-double rose, Rosa gallica officinalis, *became known for its petals, which had the ability to preserve their scent when dried. It was said that when Marie Antoinette visited Provins in 1770, a bed of rose petals was prepared for her. The Apothecary's Rose was probably one of the first European roses to be introduced to North America, and became known for its beauty and medicinal qualities.*

and with a shrublike habit, and bears yellow flowers, flushed purple, from mid- to late summer.

Jasmine: This is a slightly Oriental redolence, and one that is revealed by *Jasminum officinale*, the Common White Jasmine or Jessamine. It is a deciduous climber, with white flowers borne in lax clusters from mid- to late summer.

Sweet: Many climbers have this appealing redolence, including the Pink Jasmine, *Jasminum polyanthum*. A slightly tender semi-evergreen, it has white and pale pink flowers from late spring to midsummer. The Goat Leaf Honeysuckle,

FRAGRANCES INDOORS

Creating fragrances indoors has been pursued for thousands of years, masking unpleasant household smells and warding off germs and insect pests. It is a craft with many facets, from scented garden flowers picked to make small nosegays (earlier known as 'tussie mussies') to potpourris, moth sachets and floral waters. Here are a few of these fragrant treasures:

Potpourris: A mixture of dried flower petals and spices kept in a container and used to scent the air. They are either 'dry' or 'moist'; both create wonderful fragrances. However, the moist type is not visually attractive, while the dry type needs periodic reviving with essential oils or a proprietary reviver.

Sachets and sweet bags: Sweet-smelling flowers, spices and herbs enclosed in small, attractive bags or packages are ideal for fresh-ening and scenting linen cupboards, drawers and chests. Recipes include rose petals, crushed rosemary, powdered Orrisroot, lavender, sticks of cinnamon and essential oils.

Bath bags: An excellent way to add fragrances to baths; muslin bags with drawstring tops are filled with fragrant plants, together with powdered milk and oatmeal to soften the water and to bulk out the ingredients. The plants include rosemary, lemon balm, peppermint, orange peel, lavender, marigold and rose

petals. The sachets are suspended in the bath so that water trickles through them.

Floral waters: Many scented waters are can be made; they are less heavily scented than colognes, and can be used as toilet waters, splashes, or just refreshing pick-me-ups. They are mixtures of fragrant herbs, water and, sometimes, essential oils. Alcohol is also occasionally added.

Moth sachets: Several plants have gained fame through their ability to repel moths, including southernwood, rue, tansy and rosemary.

Scented wreaths: Wreaths have funereal connotations and are steeped in memo-rial thoughts. However, when formed of scented flowers and herbs, they assume a different role and are ideal for introduc-ing rich fragrances throughout the year. As such, they are more like garlands than wreaths.

SCENTED PRIMULAS

Several attractively scented primulas thrive in moist soil and are best planted in large groups, rather than as solitary plants dotted over a large area.

Primula beesiana develops whorls of fragrant, lilacpurple flowers on sturdy stems during early and mid- summer. Deep rooted, it needs slow, deep watering. The widely grown and popular Drumstick Primrose, *Primula denticulata*, gives densely-packed globular heads, 5–7.5 cm wide lavender-blue flowers in spring and early summer. There are rose-purple and white forms; they all have a honey fragrance. Like many primroses, it is not adapted to warm-winter regions.

The Tibetan primrose *Primula florindae*, has sweet, pale yellow, bell-shaped flowers during early and mid-summer. *Primula prolifera* (earlier called *P. helodoxa*), has golden-yellow flowers in early and midsummer.

The popular Himalayan Cowslip, *Primula sikkimensis*, has delicately sweet, pale yellow flowers borne in pendant clusters during early and midsummer.

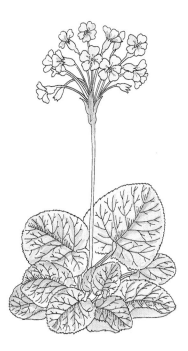

FRENCH CONNECTION

The French knew the value of southernwood, Artemisia abrotanum, *native to southern Europe, where it was known as garde robe and placed in wardrobes and drawers to keep clothes free of moths and other insects.*

Perfoliate or Italian Woodbine, *Lonicera caprifolium* is a deciduous climber with creamy white flowers, tinged pink, during midsummer. The Giant Burmese Honeysuckle, *Lonicera hildebrandiana*, also has sweetly scented flowers. It is a tender evergreen or partly deciduous climber with large, creamy white flowers during mid- and late summer. A related plant, the Japanese Honeysuckle or Gold and Silver Flower, *Lonicera japonica*, is an evergreen climber, with white to pale-yellow flowers from midsummer to autumn. The Early Dutch Honeysuckle, *Lonicera periclymenum* 'Belgica', is a deciduous climber with purplish-red and yellow flowers during early and midsummer. With a similar redolence, the common honeysuckle, *Lonicera periclymenum* 'Serotina', again deciduous, has flowers that reveal creamy-white insides and reddish-purple exteriors during mid- and late summer. Few climbers have such distinctive flowers as the Blue Crown Passion Flower, *Passiflora caerulea*. It is slightly tender, with pink-tinged white petals and blue-purple centres from early to late summer.

Sweet Pea: The ordinary Sweet Pea, *Lathyrus odoratus*, reveals this distinctive fragrance. It is a self-clinging, hardy

Above left: The slightly sweet flowers of the Common Passion Flower, *Passiflora caerulea*, create a superb display. It can be planted against a sheltered, warm wall.

Above: The vanilla-scented flowers produced by the Chinese Wisteria, *Wisteria sinensis,* are born, in large, pendulous bunches in early summer.

Fragrant rambling and climbing roses

As well drenching the air with sweetness, several roses that climb aloft have unusual bouquets.

Ramblers have long, flexible stems, often growing 3 m or more in one season, that bear clusters of many small, rosette-shaped flowers. They are ideal for clothing arches and pergolas, or rambling through trees.

Climbers, however, have a more permanent framework of branches, with flowers borne singly or in small clusters. They are ideal for growing against permanent frameworks on house walls.

Apple: Several roses have this fresh bouquet, including 'François Juranville', a rambler with coral-pink flowers, deepening towards their centres. 'René André' also has this fragrance, a rambler with small, cupped, soft apricot-yellow flowers flushed with pink. 'Paul Transon', a rambler, bears copper-orange flowers in small clusters.

Clove: 'Blush Noisette', a climber, has clusters of small, cupped, semidouble, lilac-pink flowers.

Fruity: 'Albéric Barbier' a rambler, bears yellow buds that open to double, creamy-white flowers. 'New Dawn' a climber, has silvery, blush-pink flowers that deepen towards the centre.

Lemon: 'Leverkusen', a climber, reveals rosette-shaped, lemon-yellow flowers. With a similar fragrance, *Rosa bracteata,* the Macartney Rose, is a climber, bearing large, single, silky-white flowers.

Musk: 'Aimée Vibert' is a climber that develops graceful sprays of small, double, pure white flowers with yellow stamens. The Musk Rose, *Rosa moschata,* is a climber with sprays of single, glistening white flowers.

Myrrh: The New English Rose 'Constance Spry' is sometimes grown as a climber. It develops clear pink flowers. 'Cressida', another New English Rose, has this unusual bouquet; it is often grown as a climber, and develops large, apricot-pink flowers.

Orange: This is an attractive and fresh bouquet present in the rambler 'The Garland'; it bears bunches of small, creamy salmon flowers. 'Veilchenblau', another rambler, also has this redolence

annual with well-known, pealike flowers in colours including pink, white, or purple from mid-summer to fall.

Vanilla: A couple of wisterias reveal this fragrance: the Japanese Wisteria, *Wisteria floribunda,* with large, pendulous clusters of violet-blue flowers during early summer, and the Chinese Wisteria, *Wisteria sinensis,* with mauve flowers, again during early summer. Both of them are hardy, deciduous climbers.

ANCIENT IRIS

Earlier known as *Iris florentina,* Orrisroot (*Iris germanica florentina*) has violet-scented roots that have been used for 2000 years or more in toilet preparations. Earlier, this plant was known as White Flower de Luce and Flower de Luce of Florence. The roots were lifted, cleaned, dried and ground, and used in many toilet preparations, including tooth powders. The rich and unusual bouquet increases as the roots are dried. It is now mainly used in potpourri. Medicinally, the juice of this plant has been used to treat dropsy, while in the dry state it is good for complaints of the lungs.

and displays small, crimson-purple flowers that fade to lilac.

Peony: The rambler 'Gerbe Rose' has double, quartered, soft-pink flowers tinted cream.

Primrose: 'Adeläide d'Orléans', a rambler, bears small, semi-double, creamy-white flowers. Another rambler, 'Debutante', also has this fragrance and produces sprays of small, rose-pink flowers, fading to blush. With a similar scent, 'Félicité et Perpétue', a rambler, has large clusters of pompon-like, creamy-white flowers.

Spicy: 'Dreamgirl', a climber, has rosette-shaped, coral-pink flowers.

Sweet Pea: For this redolence, plant the climber 'Mme Grégoire Staechelin', with semi-double, glowing-pink flowers.

Tea Rose: This fragrance is reminiscent of earlier years, and several climbers reveal it. 'Lady Hillingdon, Climbing' has rich apricot-yellow flowers, while 'Souvenir de la Malmaison, Climbing' develops large, globular, blush-pink flowers.

AROMATIC SHRUBS

Shrubs with aromatic leaves are always welcome in gardens, as they create exciting and unusual redolences throughout the entire year. The scents emitted by their aromatic foliage are often reminiscent of the warmth and ambience of southern Mediterranean countries.

Several popular garden shrubs have aromatic leaves and yield well-known essential oils. These include oil of rosemary (*Rosmarinus officinalis*), oil of myrtle (*Myrtus communis*) and oil of lavender

(*Lavandula stoechas*). Concentrated amounts of these oils only become available after extensive extraction, most of these shrubs, however, especially when in a warm, still position, make known the nature of their oils. Some aromatic plants, however, apparently did not need the confines of a gardens: the seventeenth-century English writer and garden designer John Evelyn tells that the fragrance of rosemary could be detected thirty leagues off the coast of Spain. (A league, by the way, is about three miles – a bold claim!)

An unusual and distinctive way to grow rosemary is in a large tub. Put five to seven very small plants in each tub, and immediately pinch out the growing points to encourage bushiness. Each spring, for the following two years, nip out the growing points from all shoots; this will keep the plants low and bushy.

Left: Sweet peas, raised each year from seed, are the epitome of a scented garden. Their relaxed style invokes thoughts of cottage gardens.

Eventually, the tub will be covered by a domelike array of foliage and flowers. Plant up two large tubs, and position them each side of your front door.

Aromatic shrubs are also ideal for planting alongside paths, and especially at their junctions, where, because of their longevity, they become points of reference and of special importance to people who are visually impaired.

Here are a few garden shrubs with aromatic foliage:

Camomile: Lavender Cotton, *Santolina chamaecyparissus,* is hardy, with aromatic, woolly, silvery, threadlike foliage. Also, it develops bright, lemon-yellow flowers during midsummer. *Santolina pinnata neapolitana* (earlier known as *S. neapolitana*), also known as Lavender Cotton, has this bouquet, too. It is a hardy shrub with feathery, grey leaves and bright lemon-yellow flowers during

midsummer. In winter, bring into a cool spot indoors in colder regions.

Curry: By name alone, the Curry Plant or White Leaf Everlasting, *Helichrysum italicum* (still better known by its early name, *H. angustifolium*), is bound to produce foliage with a curry-like redolence. It is a hardy, shrubby plant with silver-grey, needle-like leaves covered in a down that emits the aroma of curry. Attractive, mustard-yellow flowers appear from early to late summer.

Gum: The Gum Cistus or Ladanum, *Cistus ladanifer,* is a slightly tender, evergreen shrub bearing dull-green, narrow, lancelike leaves and white flowers with yellow stamens in early midsummer.

Lavender: There are several attractive lavenders, including the Old English Lavender, *Lavandula angustifolia* (earlier known as *L. spica* or *L. officinalis*). It is a hardy, evergreen shrub with silvery-grey, narrow leaves and pale, grey-blue flowers during mid- and late summer. The French Lavender or Spanish Lavender, *Lavandula stoechas,* is another hardy, evergreen shrub, with narrow, grey-green leaves and dark-purple flowers in long spikes during midsummer.

Lemon: The Lemon-scented Verbena, *Aloysia triphylla* (earlier called *Lippia citriodora*), also known as Lemon Verbena, is a slightly tender, deciduous shrub with pale- to mid-green, lance-shaped leaves that have a strong lemon bouquet when crushed. Small, tubular, pale-mauve flowers appear in late summer.

Myrtle: The true Myrtle, Greek Myrtle,

or Swedish Myrtle, *Myrtus communis,* is a slightly tender, evergreen shrub with glossy, mid-green, oval to lance-shaped leaves that have the distinctive aroma of myrtle when bruised. Small white or pink flowers appear from early to late summer.

Orange: This is always a welcome bouquet in a garden, and the Mexican Orange Bush, *Choisya ternata,* is a slightly tender, evergreen shrub with glossy, green leaves that when bruised yield the fragrance of oranges. White, orange blossom-like flowers appear during late spring and early summer.

Pungent and acrid: Rue or Herb of Grace, *Ruta graveolens,* is a well-known hardy, evergreen shrub with glaucous, bluish-green leaves and mustard-yellow flowers during mid- and late summer.

Sharp: Artemisia absinthium, variously known as Common Wormwood, Absinthe, Lad's Love and Old Man, is a soft-wooded, semi-evergreen or deciduous shrub with grey-green, downy, finely divided leaves and dull-yellow flowers during late summer and into autumn.

Wintergreen: Wintergreen, *Gaultheria procumbens* (also known as Creeping Wintergreen, Checkerberry, Teaberry, Mountain Tea and Ivy-leaves), is a hardy, evergreen shrub with shiny, dark green leaves that have the penetrating aroma of wintergreen.

SUMMER SHRUBS

Gardens abound in shrubs and trees with fragrant summer flowers. Most of them are sweetly scented, but a few have unusual scents that soon captivate the nose and make a garden more exciting and stimulating. Here are a few of these unusual fragrances:

Acrid: Warminster Broom, *Cytisus × praecox,* is a deciduous shrub with creamy-white, pea-shaped flowers during late spring and early summer.

Almond: The European Bird Cherry, *Prunus padus* 'Grandiflora', is a magnificent deciduous tree, with slender, drooping tassels packed with small, white flowers during early summer. With a similar fragrance, the Yoshino Cherry, *Prunus × yedoensis,* has white flowers in pendulous clusters during mid- and late spring.

Cowslip: This fragrance has a delicate nature, and can be found in the Buttercup Witch Hazel, *Corylopsis pauciflora,* a hardy, deciduous shrub with pale prim rose-yellow, bell-shaped flowers borne on bare stems during mid- and late spring. Another shrub with this fragrance is *Corylopsis willmottiae,* a hardy, deciduous shrub with greenish-yellow flowers in dropping clusters during mid- and late spring.

Honey: The Spanish Broom or Weaver's Broom, *Spartium junceum,* has a deciduous nature with bright, golden-yellow, pea-shaped flowers on rushlike stems during mid- and late summer.

Lemon: Magnolia sieboldii (earlier known as *M. parviflora*) is a deciduous shrub or tree with cup-shaped, pendant, white flowers with claret-coloured stamens from early to late summer.

Lily-of-the-Valley: Skimmia japonica 'Fragrans', an evergreen shrub, has small, starlike, white flowers during late spring.

Pineapple: The Moroccan Broom, *Cytisus battandieri,* is a deciduous shrub with large, upright clusters of golden-yellow flowers during early and midsummer. It is ideal when planted against a warm wall.

Spicy: A few shrubs and trees have this captivating aroma, including *Magnolia grandiflora* 'Exmouth', an evergreen tree or large shrub with richly spicy, globular, creamy-white flowers from mid- to late

Facing page: Rue, *Ruta graveolens,* has a pungent and acrid bouquet and for many years was used to purify the air, especially in courts and gaols. Medieval monks used it to counteract eyestrain, and it is still used in this way today.

Left: Raised beds and a range of containers enable disabled gardeners to create a wealth of scents in gardens. It is essential to make sure paths are firm, well drained and wide enough to accommodate wheelchairs.

Above right: The flowers of
the Late Dutch
Honeysuckle, *Lonicera
periclymenum* 'Serotina',
have an unforgettably
sweet fragrance. It is a
sprawling, deciduous
climber and form of the
well-known Woodbine or
Honeysuckle.

summer. Another is *Ribes aureum* (earlier known as *R. tenuiflorum*), commonly known as Buffalo Currant, Golden Currant and Missouri Currant, a deciduous shrub with tubular, bright-yellow flowers in drooping clusters during late spring.

Vanilla: The evergreen *Azara microphylla* is a shrub or small tree with yellow flowers during late spring. It is best planted against a warm, sunny wall.

Violet: This delicate bouquet is revealed by the deciduous *Malus coronaria* 'Charlottae', a tree with large, semi-double, pink flowers during early summer.

SCENTED FLOWER BORDERS

Most flower borders are a medley of herbaceous perennials, bulbous plants, annuals and shrubs. All of these add vibrancy and variety:

Citron: Dictamnus albus (earlier known as *Dictamnus fraxinella*), commonly known as Burning Bush, Dittany, Gas Plant and Fraxinella, is a handsome, hardy, herbaceous perennial with white, spider-like flowers during early and mid-summer.

Cloves: Baboon Flower or Baboon-root, *Babiana plicata*, is a tender, cormous plant with pale lilac-mauve flowers during early and mid-summer.

Fruit: The Dwarf Bearded Iris, *Iris pumila,* has iris-like flowers in shades of purple, white, yellow and yellow with brown tints, during mid- and late spring.

Honey: The Madonna Lily, *Lilium candidum* (also known as White Madonna Lily, Bourbon Lily and White Lily), is a hardy, basal-rooting bulb with bell-shaped, pure-white flowers with golden anthers during mid- to late summer. Also with

honey-scented flowers, pincushion flower or Sweet Scabious, *Scabiosa atropurpurea* (also known as Mournful Widow and Mourning Bride), is a hardy annual with heads of dark-crimson flowers from mid- to late summer. There are many varieties and colours.

Jasmine: The Easter Lily or Bermuda Lily, *Lilium longiflorum,* is a hardy, stem-rooting bulb with trumpet-shaped, white flowers with golden pollen during mid- and late summer.

Musk: Sweet Sultan, *Centaurea moschata,* is a hardy annual with cornflower-like heads packed with white, pink, yellow or purple flowers from early summer to autumn.

Muscari muscarimi (earlier known as *Muscari moschatum*), commonly known as Musk Hyacinth, is a hardy bulb with flowers, first tinged purple, changing to greenish-yellow and bright-yellow, during spring and early summer.

Plum: This is an unusual fragrance to find in a flower, but one revealed by *Iris graminea*, a beardless iris with flowers during early summer, showing reddish-purple falls with blue-purple veins on a white background. *Muscari racemosum* is another plant with this redolence; a hardy bulb with deep-blue flowers with white mouths in spring.

Sage: The White Sage, *Artemisia ludoviciana,* is a hardy, herbaceous perennial with aromatic leaves and yellow flowers during late summer and autumn. Dusty Miller, *Artemisia stelleriana* (popularly and widely known as, Old Woman and

Beach Wormwood), has aromatic white leaves and yellow flowers during late summer and autumn.

Vanilla: The Tree Lupin, *Lupinus arboreus,* is a spectacular, short-lived, shrubby perennial with lemon-yellow flowers from early to late summer.

GARDENS FOR THE VISUALLY IMPAIRED

Scents play an important part in the appreciation of gardens by people who are visually impaired. Plants rich in scents can be combined with those that when shaken by gentle breezes create soothing and calming sounds.

Pathways and patios

Firm-surfaced paths – preferably without steps, sharp bends or depressions that create puddles of water – are essential to engender confidence. They should also be wide enough to take at least two people walking side-by-side. Paving stones create ideal surfaces where the ground is relatively flat, but if there are gentle slopes in several directions, crazy-paving is a better choice. If possible, create a wide central strip of paving, with 23–30 cm of pea-sized shingle on either side; edge constraints will be necessary to prevent the shingle spreading over borders. This type of path enables anyone who is visually impaired to tell when the main part of a path is being walked upon.

Pergolas, rustic arches and free-standing lattices

All of these are ideal for scented climbers at a height where they can be readily appreciated, but avoid the use of climbers that have thorns, such as roses; if a shoot becomes loose, it may glance against faces and necks. Instead, when growing roses, train them up pillars positioned away from the path's edge. Many climbing and rambling roses have exciting fragrances, and it would be a pity not to plant them in the garden.

Left: Gardens specially designed to enable visually handicapped gardeners to walk among scented plants are easily constructed, even when slopes dictate the construction of terraces and steps.

HEALING SOUNDS

*Gardens abound in sounds, ranging from the rustling of leaves to the repetitive
and reassuring pitter-patter of water splashing and tumbling from fountains
and waterfalls. Birds, with their wide range of territorial and mating calls,
add further vibrancy to gardens.*

Throughout the year, gardens are full of familiar soothing sounds, from the rustle of leaves on trees to the soft crunch of crisp, fallen leaves being trod on before rain dulls their tone. Even the sound created by walking on frost-covered grass can be soothing and gentle, perhaps offering a reminder of ever-changing seasons.

The repetitious but lively sound of water splashing from a fountain or trickling over a series of waterfalls is always soothing and comforting, especially during hot summers when it helps to create the impression that the temperature is lower than it actually is.

THE INFLUENCE OF SOUND

Sounds markedly affect our lives and few people would not agree that gardens, with their wide range of natural sounds – whether from wind, rain or animals – influence our health and vitality. Even the quiet stillness in winter after snow canopies trees, shrubs and lawns, can be reassuring, helping to reduce stress and creating a contemplative ambience.

In addition to natural sounds, it is claimed the 'shapes' of words can affect us. For instance, the sound 'O', when viewed on an instrument called a tonoscope, creates a perfectly spherical pattern, and when combined with the sound of 'M' forms a basic and important sound within many cultures. In sonic forms of yoga, 'OM' or 'AUM' is a sound claimed to be the basis of everything; Buddhists, Tibetans, Japanese, Indonesians and the Chinese view 'OM' in a similar way.

The science of sound therapy

The medicinal and scientific use of sound therapy involves the use of electronic equipment to generate sound waves that are delivered by an applicator placed over the part of the body needing treatment.

Sound therapy has been used to treat many medical problems, including rheumatoid arthritis, muscular conditions, fibrositis, bone disorders, sprains and strains. Treating problems in this way requires specialist knowledge and equipment, but encouraging a soothing array of sounds in gardens is something we all can pursue.

Attracting birds into gardens

Even gardeners who are not keen ornithologists and are unable to distinguish between a sparrow and a sea eagle usually express an interest in a bird that comes close to them. A worm or insect-hunting bird can be good company when a vegetable garden or flower border

Facing page: Garden ponds and small rock pools create tranquillity and the opportunity for reflection and contemplation. The ever changing patterns of the water, combined with the activities of fish and other water creatures, introduce vibrancy and life to the area.

Above centre: Water, whether in a garden pond or as small droplets falling off a leaf, never fails to attract attention.

CHATTERING BIRDS FOR GARDENS

Throughout the world, birds envelop gardens in nature's sounds, repeating their calls and warnings, which eventually become woven into our lives. As well as their repeated and variable twitterings, having wildlife birds in a garden adds interest, and is often a comfort for those living on their own.

is being dug, and the twitterings this interloper may offer are additional evidence of its desire to be companionable – at least while food is available!

A wide range of garden birds can be attracted by birdbaths and food. Scattering food on a raised, flat board (out of reach of cats) or hanging feeders from trees encourages many birds, including colourful members of the tit family. In North America, chickadees are similar and search out food in gardens.

Bird songs are unique to individual species, and can serve as territorial claims, flight, alarm or contact calls, as well as ways to attract mates. For these reasons,

many birds sing only in spring and early summer, and they often have a characteristic way of delivering their songs. The nightingale likes to be hidden, while the icterine warbler prefers exposure. Others, like the white-throat, sing while in flight.

ATTRACTING BEES INTO GARDENS

The buzz of bees around flowers during summer is reassuring to some gardeners but alarming to others, especially if fearful of being stung. But this usually happens only when a bee is trapped or the hive threatened. Mostly, they just fly from plant to plant, happily collecting pollen.

When seeking nectar, bees pass from one plant to another, but it is mainly plants with blue flowers – and, to a lesser extent, yellow – that they visit. This is because although bees are able to see most colours, they are unable to distinguish red from green, and both appear to be grey. Blue-flowered plants such as *Lobelia erinus* (Edging Lobelia or Trailing Lobelia), *Anchusa azurea, Aster novi-belgii* (Michaelmas Daisy), *Scabiosa caucasica* and *Tradescantia virginiana* (Common Spiderwort or Widow's-tears) have special appeal to them.

Incidentally, it has been discovered that worker bees when returning to a hive and laden with nectar are able to communicate to other bees the location of the plant bearing the pollen.

MUSICAL TREES AND SHRUBS

Trees which shed their leaves each autumn are ideal for creating a 'rustling' garden. Evergreen types do not produce such crispness of sound, and cannot, of course, offer the bonus of richly coloured leaves in the autumn.

Large-leafed trees, such as horse chestnuts and ashes, are not always the most musical; the smaller-leafed ones, like beech, are better.

Quaking aspens

Aspens are superb at quivering, even in the slightest breeze. Although they do not create such a trill as some trees, the way they shimmer in the light is a bonus. There are several to choose from.

Variously known as White Poplar, Silver-leafed Poplar and Abele, *Populus alba* is an impressive deciduous tree, 12 m or more high, and with shallowly lobed, grey-green leaves.

Known as the Aspen, *Populus tremula* is a deciduous tree, usually 10 m high, with long, slender, flattened stalks that allow leaves to flutter even in the slightest breeze.

The Quaking Aspen, *Populus tremuloides* (also known as the Trembling Aspen, Quiverleaf, Golden Aspen and American Aspen), forms a deciduous tree, often 12 m or more high, with nearly circular, lustrous green leaves.

Ornamental grasses

Several perennial grasses create tall screens of stems and leaves that rustle in even the slightest breeze.

The Amur Silver Grass, *Miscanthus saccharjflorus,* is herbaceous and grows up to 3 m in one season, creating a superb screen for privacy and shelter; the dead stems and leaves remain through out most of the winter. The long, narrow, mid-green leaves develop from tall stems that do not need any support. There are several smaller forms, including 'Aureus' (1.5 m high, with leaves striped gold) and 'Variegatus' (1.5 m high, displaying white-striped leaves).

The herbaceous grass *Miscanthus sinensis* 'Purpureus' (sometimes known as 'Purpurascens') grows to about 1.5 m high, with erect, purplish-tinged stems bearing small leaves.

Zebra Grass, *Miscanthus sinensis* 'Zebrinus', is herbaceous and grows up to 1.2 m high, with arching, yellow-cross-banded leaves.

Bamboo screens and walks

Bamboos, also members of the grass family, are superb for creating areas of rustling leaves. They are hardy in temperate regions, and ideal for forming a 'bamboo walk' of different species, perhaps either side of a gravel path which, when trodden on, adds a further sound dimension.

Phyllostachys nigra (earlier known as *Sinarundinaria nigra*) develops black canes up to 4.5 m tall, with narrow, 13 cm long and 2.5 cm wide leaves. It is a hardy bamboo that needs plenty of space.

Pleioblastus variegatus (earlier known as *Arundinaria variegata* and *Sasa variegata*)

WIND CHIMES

The gentle, repetitive yet unpredictable sounds of wind chimes are known throughout many countries, where they create light background sounds, comforting in their repetition, and ideal for reducing stress.

grows to 1.2 m high and forms a thicket of stems with narrowly oblong and lance-shaped leaves. They are up to 20 cm long, mid-green, and striped white. It is ideal for planting alongside a path.

Pseudosasa japofmica (earlier and still better known as *Arundinaria japonica*) forms a thicket of stems up 3–5 m high, with dark, glossy-green, sharp-pointed leaves up to 30 cm long. It is one of the hardiest bamboos.

Sasa veitchii, low-growing and thicket-forming, has canes 1–1.2 m high and rich, deep green leaves up to 25 cm long. The tips and edges of the leaves tend to wither during winter. It is ideal for planting alongside a path.

Sinarundinaria nitida (earlier known as *Arundinaria nitida*) grows up to 2.5 m high, with a mass of purple stems. Its leaves are narrowly lance-shaped and

Left: Grasses introduce the gentle and repetitive sound of rustling into gardens whenever the wind blows. There are many grasses to choose from, including *Miscanthus sinensis* 'Variegatus'.

EARLY AMERICAN FOUNTAIN

Indoor water gardens became fashionable during the mid 1800s. This illustration of a cast-iron plant stand first appeared in the American Gardeners' Monthly *and later was reproduced in* The Cottage Gardener *in 1860.*

Above right: Water garden features need not be large. Here, a low-powered pump produces a small, plume-like fountain in a large pot. It is a feature that can be introduced into most gardens – even those created on a small patio.

water pressure, water had to be pumped from the River Seine.

Islamic gardens were not so concerned with the use of water in such artificial ways, and concentrated on the element itself, using both large and small areas of still, quiet water. However, by the time the Islamic faith reached Spain, fountains became an important part of many gardens.

Chinese gardens were mainly devoid of fountains, as they preferred to use water in its natural state, although in the eighteenth century a garden built by Jesuits near Beijing for Ch'ien Lung contained fountains and jets of water.

Like the Chinese, the Japanese preferred to use water in a natural way, although they did include cascades in their gardens.

Using fountains today

Most early fountains depended on a reservoir of water – whether natural or artificial – high above the fountain to create pressure and an attractive display. Although a wide variety of pumps are available for fountains and waterfalls today, they fall into two basic types.

Submersible pumps are designed to be totally submerged in a pond, and to work silently. They are best positioned on a raised plinth in the pond's base to prevent them being covered by silt. Most are powered by mains electricity through low-voltage transformers. The installation must include a ground fault circuit interrupter (GFCI) which quickly turns off the power supply if a fault occurs

features, originated in Babylonian gardens, were used, including those for amusement as well as function.

The Romans used fountains both indoors and outside; Pliny the Younger, in the first century AD, wrote of a fountain indoors so that diners could hear the water falling, while outdoor fountains often played among the vines.

Renaissance gardens, which began in the late fifteenth century, revived classical ideas of villas and the use of water, and many courtyards in Italy and France were adorned with tiered fountains with water flowing from the edges of one bowl into a larger one beneath. Using water in the grand style perhaps reached its peak with the fountains of Versailles, where, unlike the grand water-gardens in Italy, which often had hilltop streams to guarantee in the cables or pump. The size of the pump needed for each pond will depend on the number and size of fountains, if any.

Surface pumps are necessary when a large volume of water is required to allow a continuous supply to several fountains and a waterfall. Depending on the type of pump, it may need to be primed before use. Surface pumps need to be housed in a cool, waterproof, accessible chamber.

Before selecting the type of pump, consult with a specialist company. As an indication of the type of pump needed, for a fountain creating spray up to 1.2 m high, a low-voltage submersible pump is suitable, but where a spray of water 2.2 m high is needed, a mains submersible type is best. For sprays over this height, a surface pump is essential. Never economize on the pump's size and power, especially if you intend to add an additional water feature at a later date. Also, remember that using a long piece of small-bore piping to transfer water from the pump to the pond can seriously reduce the flow.

Always seek the advice of a specialist before installing electricity outdoors.

Types of fountains

Various spray patterns that can be created by fountains, ranging from those that form single or multiple columns of water to ones with a bell, tulip or hemispherical outline. But before selecting one, there are a few practical considerations:

The height of the spray should rise to no more than half the pond's width. Always make sure that the type of spray suits the pond's nature and does not dominate it.

Position the fountain so the spray does not fall on water lilies. Also, check that the spray does not push floating plants all over the pond's surface.

In windy areas, use fountains that produce large droplets of water, because these will not spread as far when blown by the wind; also, nozzles with fine holes are more likely to become blocked than larger ones. However, fine water droplets cause less damage to water lilies than coarse types.

Keep filters clean so there is a constant supply of water to the fountain.

UNUSUAL FOUNTAINS

Where space is limited, small fountains that squirt water from the mouths of plaster animals such as lions and dogs, as well as cherubs and young clowns, help to create interest in ponds at ground level as well as in raised ponds.

CURATIVE CATTAILS

Native to parts of North America as well as other areas of the world, the moisture-loving Common Cattail (Typha latifolia) *and Narrow-leafed Cattail* (T. angustifolia) *have many uses. The roots were made into flour, while in spring fresh, young shoots were peeled and eaten raw or cooked.*

The leaves are used to weave mats and to make baskets and chair seats.

Native Americans have used the soft, downlike material which can be stripped from the seedheads to make absorbent pads to dress wounds and burns.

PATHS AND OTHER SURFACES

The sounds created by walking on paths can be reassuring and comforting. Smooth paving slabs produce an even and strong surface that can be relied upon, while natural stone paving has an uneven surface, which means that more care is needed when walking on it.

Gravels of all shapes, sizes, and colours have become popular, and these produce a variety of sounds when walked on. Some are reminiscent of former walks, perhaps during childhood holidays and along stony beaches. Because gravels are noisy to tread on, they soon reveal the presence of people, and many people consider them useful in revealing the presence of any intruders.

HERBS FOR HEALING

Employing plants to cure illness has long been part of many cultures, and their selection and use was earlier attributed to the gods. It was believed that poisonous plants harboured evil spirits, whereas curative ones were the abodes of benevolent spirits.

About 1500 BC, the ancient Egyptians reached the peak of their civilization and are said to have had about 700 remedies, using plants such as mint, caraway, dill, aniseed, fennel and sesame. The practical application of herbal medicines was refined by the Egyptians: carriers for liquid doses were water, honey, wine and beer, while pills and pastilles were also developed. Suppositories were widely used, and for external application, poultices and ointments were known. They even knew the value of inhalation, producing vapours by pouring liquids on hot stones.

Knowledge of plants and their application was passed to learned Greek writers and botanists. One of the earliest of these was Theophrastus (*c*.370–*c*.286 BC), who lived on the island of Lesbos. He succeeded Aristotle in the government of the School at Athens, and is the earliest known European botanical author. Theophrastus was a keen observer of plants and life in general, and it is likely that some of his writings originated from Aristotle.

In AD 23–79, the Roman author Gaius Plinius Secundus (better known as Pliny the Elder, who lost his life when going to the aid of friends threatened by the eruption of Vesuvius) wrote *Naturalis, Historia,* an extensive work of 37 books.

Dioscorides, a doctor who lived in Anazarba in Cilicia, Asia Minor, during the first century AD, wrote *Materia Medica,* which is considered to be a valuable source of early medicinal plants. The renowned Roman physician Galen (Galenos) lived from AD *c*.130–*c*.200, and wrote many medical books.

RELIGION AND MEDICINE

During the later days of ancient Egypt, decadence led to magic and priests assuming dominance over the earlier learned and reasoned use of herbal medicine. Illness was assumed to be the result of evil spirits and a manifestation of wrongs perpetrated by a patient. Gradually, a bleak period in medical thought developed, which continued all the way through to the end of the seventeenth century, when medicine was described as being mostly composed of a mixture of white magic, witchcraft and religion. Indeed, in the eighteenth century, Voltaire, the French philosopher, historian and dramatist, said it was like 'pouring medicine of which they knew little into bodies of which they knew less'.

Herbs and the Dark Ages

For many centuries – from about AD 500 to the beginning of the Renaissance – Europe was engulfed in the so-called Dark Ages, when learning and original

Facing page: This twelfth-century Arab manuscript from a *Book of Antidotes* shows a doctor preparing an antidote to a snake bite.

Above centre: The well-known puffball-like seedhead of the Common Dandelion, *Taraxacum officinale.* It is native to wide areas of the northern hemisphere, in pastures, meadows and wastelands. Many parts are used medicinally: an infusion of fresh roots is good in the treatment of gallstones, jaundice and other liver problems, while the leaves ease chronic rheumatism, gout and stiff joints.

MONASTIC HERBS

A herb garden illustrated in a 1490 book published in Venice. In the Middle Ages, monasteries became repositories for herbs, and many herbal illustrations date from that era.

Above right: This is part of a cartouche from *Historia Naturalis*, published about 1460 in Siena, a cathedral town in central Italy. It shows two gardeners in a leafy arbour. There appear to be several trees growing up and over the arbour, with a climber curling around one of them, The gardener on the right has a spade with edges sheathed in metal to give greater durability.

Elizabethan herbalists – and later

Many well-known English herbalists lived in or about the Elizabethan period, mainly during the latter part of the sixteenth century. A few of them translated Greek and Latin herbals into English, which when viewed from today's perceptive have a quaint, pleasing and poetic nature.

John Gerard (also spelt Gerarde and Gerrard) was born in Cheshire, England, in 1545, later journeying to London and settling in Holborn. He became a barber-surgeon in 1569, and Master of the Company of Barber-Surgeons about eight years later. He was an enthusiastic botanist, and published his best-known work – *Herball, or general histoirie of plantes* – in 1597. It was revised by the apothecary Thomas Johnson in 1633, 21 years after Gerard's death in 1612.

John Parkinson, a contemporary of

thought were often associated with the devil. Knowledge of herbs was widely looked upon as evidence of paganism and mysticism. However, an understanding of herbs was kept alive by monks in the seclusion of monasteries, where herbals were occasional compiled about their cultivation and use. Towards the end of the Dark Ages, more monks took up the cultivation of herbs so that they could administer to the bodily as well as the spiritual needs of their flocks. Physick gardens became essential parts of monasteries and, later, courts and hospitals.

The distillation of herbs became important in the production of medicines, and early attempts at distillation were performed in alembics (vessels with a beaked head or cap).

DOCTRINE OF SIGNATURES

During the early sixteenth century, the Doctrine of Signatures – a development of mimetic magic (like suggesting like) – was popularized by the Swiss-German physician and alchemist Paracelsus (1493–1541). The philosophy he prescribed said that the medicinal value of any natural substance is indicated by its character. For example, a plant's shape or colour was held to indicate its medicinal use. This indication of use was thought to be the

signature or stamp of a guardian angel.

The logic of this philosophy suggested that the spotted leaves of lungwort, *Pulmonaria officinalis* (*left*), were a cure for pulmonary complaints, that plants with yellow flowers or roots with yellow sap controlled jaundice, and red-coloured roots were ideal for blood disorders. This ancient philosophy was followed by many well-known early herbalists.

Gerard, was born in 1567 and died in 1650. He was a gardener and herbalist, trained as an apothecary, and wrote several well-known books – *Paradisi in Sole, Paradisus Terrestris* in 1629, mainly devoted to plants for pleasure, and his herbal *Theatrurn Botanicurn, A Herball of a Large Extent* in 1640, with descriptions of about 3800 plants.

The now world-famous herbalist Nicholas Culpeper published the first edition of his famous book the *English Physician* in 1652; later, it became known as his *Herbal*. He was born in 1616, studied at Cambridge, and when aged 24 set up as an astrologer-physician in Spitalfields, London.

Culpeper developed the philosophy that heavenly bodies – the stars, sun, moon and planets – have a great influence on plants. His herbal set out his method of astrological diagnosis, which involved considering the planet that governed the afflicted part, then selecting plants governing the opposite planet to heal the ailment. In 1654, Culpeper died of consumption at the early age of 38.

Modern herbalists

One of the most comprehensive herbals of recent years has been *A Modern Herbal*, published in 1931 and written by Mrs M. Grieve. It was edited and introduced by Mrs C. F. Leyel, who for many years was Director of the Society of Herbalists. Before the herbal's publication, Mrs Leyel

was asked to make sure that North American herbs were included, and the result was a tome of some 900 pages and

DEMONIC MANDRAKE

Also known as Devil's Apples, Mandragora officinarum *(earlier called* Atropa mandragora*) is steeped in folklore as well as medicinal powers. The plant was said to grow under the gallows of murderers, and to utter shrieks that caused death when pulled from the soil. Sometimes dogs were tethered to the plant, so that they pulled it up, risking death themselves.*

Left: Pepper (*Piper nigrum*), indigenous to moist, low-country forest areas of Asia, is a creeping, perennial vine. This illustration in the fifteenth-century *Livre des Merveilles* (*Book of Miracles*) shows peppers being harvested in the Kingdom at Quilon, on the south-west tip of India. Regarded as 'black gold' in the Middle Ages, herbalists may still recommend it for ringworm.

information on more than 1000 British and American herbal plants. The book has reprinted frequently and is still in print.

MEDICINAL HERBS

Plants with medicinal qualities grow throughout the world and have markedly contributed to our health and well being. Indigenous peoples made use of them, and every country's folklore is steeped in stories of their use.

Native Americans and Mexicans knew the value of the shrubby *Ephedra umevadenis*, which, when formed into a tea, cured colds, fevers and headaches, while in cold, snowy, northern regions the roots of Scurvy Grass (a roseroot – so named because its edible roots, when crushed, smell of roses) provided vitamin C and helped to prevent scurvy.

ALEMBIC OVENS

Early distillation was performed in alembic ovens, and by the end of the sixteenth century there were many designs – here are a few.

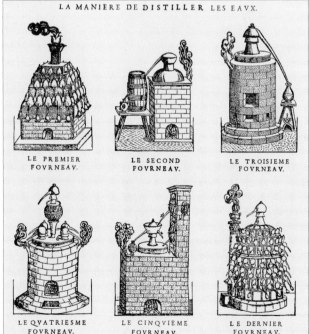

LA MANIERE DE **DISTILLER** LES EAVX.

LE PREMIER FOVRNEAV.

LE SECOND FOVRNEAV.

LE TROISIEME FOVRNEAV.

LE QVATRIESME FOVRNEAV.

LE CINQVIEME FOVRNEAV.

LE DERNIER FOVRNEAV.

ORDEAL POISONS

In former times, people suspected of witchcraft and other crimes were made to swallow poison to test their guilt or innocence. If the person died, it was taken as on indication of guilt, while if the poison was vomited, they were held to be innocent. Poisons from several trees were used:

Antiaris toxicaria (Upas Tree, Riti, Ordeal Tree of Java, Hypo, Pohon Upas, Antsjar or Sack Tree) is a tree said to give off poisonous fumes fatal to all animal life. The sap contains a poison known as ipoh, which was used to tip poisoned arrows.

Cerbera tanghin (Tanghin Poison, or Ordeal Poison Tree of Madagascar) forms a small tree with milky sap used as a poison.

Erythrophleum suaveolens (earlier known as *E. guineense*, and commonly known as Sassy Bark, Ordeal Tree of Sierra Leone or Casca Bark), is a tree with poisonous bark formerly used in ordeal trials; it is also used as on arrow poison.

Excaecaria agallocha (Blinding Tree, Agallocha, or Talo-kiriya) is a small tree with milky, acrid juice which blisters skin

NIGERIA
calabar

AFRICA

in ordeal tests; it has also been used in the treatment of leprosy.

Hippomane mancinella (Manchineal Tree) is a poison- ous swamp tree of tropical South America and West Indian islands, with poisonous, acrid, milky juice. It is said that even grass will not grow underneath this tree.

Physostigma venenosum (Calabar Bean, Ordeal Bean of Old Calabar or Chop Nut) is a twining climber with large, dark-brown seeds.

The roots of *Cimicjfuga racemosa* (widely known as Black Snake Root, Squaw Root and Bugbane) were used as an antidote against poison and the bite of the rattlesnake, while *Erythronium americanum* (Yellow Adder's Tongue or Amberwell), formed a stimulating poultice and was applied to tumours, swellings and ulcers.

Celtic tribes in Britain used woad as a body dye to frighten their enemies, as well as to treat ulcers, inflammation and to staunch bleeding. The Maoris of New Zealand used the bark of miro, *Podocarpus*

ferrugineus, to assist in healing wounds and ulcers, while in India the Thorn Apple, *Datura alba,* is still employed to treat asthma, coughing fits in whooping cough and spasms of the bladder.

Many herbs have medicinal uses:

Aconite (Aconitum napellus), a herbaceous perennial native to Europe and Asia, has a multitude of other names including Monkshood, Friar's Cap, Helmet Flower and Wolfsbane. The roots and leaves are used medicinally in the treatment of scarlatina, gastritis, facial neuralgia, catarrh, tonsillitis and croup. It is a poisonous plant and must be treated with respect.

Angelica (*Angelica archangelica*), native in many European countries, is a sturdy, hardy biennial or short-lived perennial with roots, stems and seeds used medicinally as an antidyspeptic, for flatulence and to ease rheumatic pain. Earlier, roots were used to combat typhoid.

Anise (*Pimpinella anisum*), native to southern Europe, Egypt and the Near East, is also known as aniseed. It is a hardy annual with greyish or brownish-grey seeds used in cough medicine and lozenges. The seeds are also used in confectionery and to enhance the flavour of meat.

Belladonna (*Atropa belladonna*), also known as Dwale, Deadly Nightshade, Naughty Man's Cherries and Great Morel, is native to a wide area including Europe, western Asia to Iran, and North Africa. It is a perennial that produces a narcotic used to treat night-sweats, coughs, whooping-cough, gout and rheumatic inflammations. Belladonna is also widely used in the treatment of eye problems. All parts of the plant are extremely poisonous and should not be touched with hands that have abrasions!

Bistort (*Polygonum bistorta*), a herbaceous perennial native to Europe and parts of central Asia, is also known as Snakeweed, Easter Ledges, Easter Mangiant, Adderwort and Twice Writhen. Its roots are used medicinally to treat haemorrhages and mucus discharges.

DANGEROUS LAUGHTER!

The Saffron Crocus, Crocus sativus, *has a long history and was used by the Arabs, Mongols and Greeks. The Romans used saffron extensively, as a medicine, condiment, disinfectant and dye. Its medicinal value has been to help digestion, strengthen the stomach, to cleanse the lungs and to control coughs. However, when used excessively it is known to cause uncontrollable laughter.*

Above left: Woad (*Isatis tinctoria*) was earlier grown for the dye extracted from its leaves. Medicinally, it has been prepared as a paste and applied to the area over the spleen, and used to treat ulcers and to ease inflammation.

TREATING ANIMALS

Herbs have also played a role in keeping animals healthy, and many have continued to be used in homoeopathy for both farm and domestic animals. Homoeopathy uses a very small dose of a medicinal substance – possibly a poison – which in a larger dose would cause symptoms similar to the illness being treated. These are prepared in such a way as to make them very safe. The range of plants used in homoeopathy is extensive and includes the following:

Arnica montana (Arnica or Mountain Tobacco) counteracts physical trauma such as shock after road accidents, blows, falls, bruising, bite wounds, surgery and cerebral hemorrhages.

Atropa belladonna (Belladonna or Deadly Nightshade) eases heat-stroke when the sun's rays are low.

Gelsemium sempervirens (Conium, Yellow Jasmine or Wild Woodbine) eases emotional excitement that may lead to bodily ailments.

Strychnos ignatii (Ignatia) helps in the treatment of an animal that pines for its owner. Take care, as it is very poisonous!

Datura stramonium (Stramonium, Thorn Apple, Jimson Weed or Stinkweed) assists in treating cats that have developed the habit of wetting in the house.

Symphyturn officinale (Symphytum, Comfrey, Knitback or Boneset) helps fractures to unite and heal.

Urtica urens (Stinging Nettle) aids in regulation of milk secretion.

All medicines given to animals must be prescribed by a qualified veterinary surgeon.

Several of its common names refer to its snake-like, twisted roots.

Blood Root (*Sanguinaria canadensis*) is a North American and Canadian herbaceous perennial also known as Red Root, Tetterwort, Indian Paint, Red Pucoon, Sweet Slumber, Coon Root and Snakebite. Medicinally, the rhizomes (root part) have been used as a tonic, stimulant and expectorant. Native Americans have used the roots to stain their bodies and clothing.

Burdock (*Arctium lappa*), a deep-rooted biennial found in Europe and Asia Minor, has several other common names including Lappa, Lappa Minor, Thorny

PERSIAN HERBALIST

A fifteenth-century engraving of a Persian herbalist. Ancient Persia (now Iran) produced some of the most advanced philosophers and herbalists of their time.

Right: Pot Marigold (*Calendula officinalis*) is a hardy annual. It is one of the most effective vulnerary (wound healing) plants. The gummy end shoots and flowers are infused in alcohol for three weeks, then strained. A few drops of this tincture added to cooled, boiled water makes the herbal equivalent of an antiseptic.

ARROW POISONS

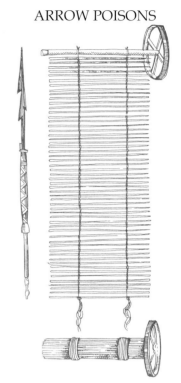

Tipping arrows with poison to cause rapid death to animals has long been practiced.

Acokanthera spectabilis (African Arrow Poison) is a large shrub. Its milky juice is extracted from its roots and shoots.

Strophanthus hispidus (White-woolly Kombe Bean or Gaboon Arrow Poison) is a woody climber native to tropical Africa with seeds that, when ripe, contain a poison used to tip arrows.

Strychnos tieute (False Upas Tree, Upas Radja, Pokroe or Tshettik), a Javanese tree, has a virulent poison extracted from its roots.

Strychnos toxifera (Curare, Curari, Urari or Wourali poison) is a South American poisonous tree; extracts derived from the bark are used to tip arrows.

Tabernaemontana malaccensis (Prachek) is a large Malaysian shrub with milky juice used to tip arrows.

Burr, Beggar's Buttons, Love Leaves and Clot-Bur. It is claimed to be one of the finest blood purifiers, and has been used to control eczema.

Button Snakeroot (*Liatris spicata*), a hardy, tuberous, herbaceous perennial native to North America, is also known as Button Feather and Gaystar on account of its bright flower heads. Other names are Colic Root and Devil's Bite. It is a diuretic and stimulant, and is used in the treatment of such diverse problems as sore throats and gonorrhea. The related *Liatris squarrosa* has been used to treat rattlesnake bites.

Caraway (*Carum carvi*), a hardy European biennial, produces bright brown seeds used as a carminative, to provoke urine, ease colds and act as a poultice to reduce bruising. In kitchens, the seeds are used in cakes and buns and to add flavour to cabbage dishes.

Camomile (*Chamaemelum nobile*, earlier known as *Anthemis nobilis*), a European perennial with pleasantly scented leaves, also known as Roman Camomile, Double Camomile and Maythen, has flowers which are used medicinally as a tea to treat nervous and hysterical affections. Its other medicinal applications include its use as a poultice for allaying pains. As a lotion it has been used to treat earache, neuralgia, and toothache. Earlier, Camomile was used as a strewing herb.

Coolwort (*Tiarella cordifolia*), a North American ground-covering perennial also known as Foam Flower and Mitrewort, acts as a tonic and diuretic. It is also an aid

to digestion, helps dyspepsia and counteracts excess acid in the stomach.

Coriander (*Coriandrum sativum*), a hardy annual native to Asia, has seeds with medicinal values as a carminative and stimulant, It has also been used to prevent griping, and in kitchens the seeds are used to flavour curries and stews; the leaves,

often called cilantro in the United States, are used to flavour stocks and soups.

Cramp Bark (*Viburnum opulus*), a deciduous shrub native throughout much of Europe and in north and west Asia, is also known by a wealth of other common names, including High Cranberry, Guelder Rose, Snowball Tree,

COMFIT CHEST

During the fifteenth and sixteenth centuries, comfit (also known as confect) boxes were where medicines were kept. Medicinal plants such as almonds, anise, caraway, cinnamon, cloves, coriander, fennel, ginger, nutmeg and pepper were used with honey and saffron to create sugary pastilles.

Left: The Foxglove (*Digitalis purpurea*) had been used as a cardiac tonic by herbalists long before its properties were validated by scientific research. The spires of thimblelike flowers appear in early and midsummer.

**CHELSEA
PHYSIC GARDEN**

*This world-renowned garden
was founded in 1673 by the
Society of Apothecaries so
that medicinal plants could
be grown and demonstrated.
This illustration shows the
garden in 1751.*

King's Crown, Whitsun Rose, Whitten Tree and Water Elder. There is also a form, 'Americanum', that grows in Canada and the United States. An infusion or decoction of the bark was used to ease cramp and spasms, convulsion, lock-jaw and palpitations.

Digitalis (*Digitalis purpurea*), a hardy biennial native to western Europe, is also known as Fairy's Glove, Fairy Thimbles, Dead Men's Bells and Foxglove (the name 'foxglove' is said to derive from the Anglo-Saxon 'foxes-glew', an ancient musical instrument with hanging bells). The leaves have medicinal powers as a cardiac tonic and sedative, and must be used with care. It also has a use in urinary suppression.

Dill (*Anethum graveolens*, earlier known as *Peucedanum graveolens*), a hardy annual, has seeds with medicinal properties for easing swellings and pains, as well as a remedy for flatulence and digestive upsets. In kitchens, the seeds are added to vinegar for pickling gherkins, and fresh leaves are used to garnish fish dishes, new potatoes and peas.

Dyer's Weed (*Genista tinctoria*), a slender-stemmed, deciduous shrub native to Europe and west and northern Asia, is also called Dyer's Greenweed, Woadwaxen and Dyer's Broom. Twigs and leaves are used to create a medicine to combat oedema, gout and rheumatism.

Echinacea (*Echinacea angustifolia*), a North American herbaceous perennial also known as Purple Coneflower and Black Sampson, has roots which, when dried, produce a medicine that increases the body's resistance to infection. It is used to counteract a wide range of ills, from boils and septicaemia to syphilis and impurities of the blood. It is also said to have aphrodisiac qualities. Related plants also claimed to have medicinal properties are *E. purpurea* and *E. pallida*.

Elder (*Sambucus nigra*), a deciduous European tree also known as Black Elder,

European Elder, and Bour Tree, has bark, flowers and berries used medicinally. An infusion of flowers or bark has been used to treat epilepsy, while hot elderberry wine was a remedy for colds.

Fennel (*Foeniculum vulgare*), a hardy European perennial also known as Fenkel and Sweet Fennel, has seeds used to ease or remove lethargy, giddiness, headaches, palsy, sciatica and cramp. The leaves are used in salads and fish dishes.

Henbane (*Hyoscyamus niger*), a European plant with both an annual and biennial nature, also known as Henbell, Hogbean and Jupiter Bean, has soft, woolly, thick leaves with medicinal qualities. They are able to cool inflammation on the body, while earlier, when boiled in wine, they were used to treat pains in joints and gout. It is a very poisonous plant, and must only be used on medical advice, and never internally!

Liquorice (*Glycyrrhiza glabra*), a deep-rooted European and Asian herbaceous perennial, also known as licorice, has greyish-brown roots well known in treatments for coughs and chest and throat complaints. It was a well-known cure more than three centuries BC in the treatment of dry coughs.

Lobelia (*Lobelia inflata*), a North American annual also known as Indian Tobacco, Pukeweed, Asthma Weed, Gagroot, Vomitwort and Bladderpod, is a stimulant and expectorant, and has been useful in the treatment of whooping cough, asthma and croup. Oil of lobelia has also been useful in treating tetanus.

Peony (*Paeonia officinalis*), a herbaceous perennial native to a wide area from France to Albania, is also known as a Paeony and Piney, and is used to control convulsive and spasmodic nervous problems, including chorea, cramps, epilepsy and spasms.

Pennyroyal (*Mentha pulegium*), a European perennial also known as Pulegium, Run-by-the-Ground, Pudding Grass and Lurk-in-the-Ditch, is a member of the mint family, and when mixed with honey and salt is claimed to void phlegm from the lungs and to purge the bowels.

Also, when bruised and mixed with vinegar, it removes marks from bruising on the face and eyes and cleans ulcers. Additional uses are in treating oedema, jaundice and whooping cough.

Peppermint (*Mentha piperita*), a perennial also known as Brandy Mint, Curled Mint, and Balm Mint, is an astringent and strengthener of the stomach, aiding in the treatment of nausea, looseness and retching.

Poppy (*Papaver somniferum*), a hardy annual native to western Asia and widely known as the Opium Poppy, White Poppy

THE DEADLY OLEANDER

The oleander or Rose Bay (Nerium oleander) *is often grown as a houseplant in temperate countries but in Mediterranean countries it develops into an evergreen shrub 3 m or more high. However, all parts are said to be extremely poisonous: during the Peninsular Wars in the early 1800s, French soldiers used oleander wood to make skewers for meat; sadly, several of them died.*

Left: The herbaceous perennial Peony (*Paeonia officianalis*) is both a magnificent garden plant and a repository of medicines in the treatment of a wide range of problems, from cramp to epilepsy.

and Mawseed, has been grown for thousands of years for its medicinal properties. Opium is derived from the milky juice of the plant and has been employed to relax nerves, and abate cramps and spasmodic complaints. It should only be used under medical direction!

Psyllium (*Plantago psyllium*), a Mediterranean perennial, also known as Flea Seed, Fleawort, Psyllium Seeds, Psyllion and Psyllios, has greyish-brown, boat-shaped seeds used to lubricate the intestine and to stimulate its natural activity. It is used in the tropics to control dysentery.

Valerian (*Valerian officinalis*), a perennial native to Europe, temperate Asia and Japan, has rhizomes used medicinally to ease nervous debility and irritation, and also to promote sleep.

Violet (*Viola odorata*), also known as Sweet Violet and Blue Violet, is a diminutive perennial native to a wide area including Europe, Asia Minor, Caucasus, Palestine and North Africa. The leaves have an antiseptic value, while the flowers are used to create a syrup to combat colds and coughs.

Wintergreen (*Gaultheria procumbens*), is a ground-creeping, evergreen shrub native to the north-east, also known as Teaberry, Boxberry, Chickerberry, Checkerberry and Partridge Berry. The leaves are used medicinally, and create a remedy for rheumatism; it is also used to control diarrhoea and as a carminative for children.

CULINARY HERB GARDENS

Many culinary herbs are native to warm countries and therefore need a sheltered aspect that slightly slopes towards the sun, to provide warmth and soil that is well drained; position plants that thrive in moist ground at the lower part of the slope.

Moderate fertility is needed, but not so rich as to produce soft, lush growth. In fact, herbs especially grown for their seeds do not need rich soil.

SHEEP BEWARE !

The leaves of the North American evergreen shrub Kalmia latifolia *are deadly to sheep. This handsome shrub is also known as spoonwood, because Native Americans carved spoons from the roots. When newly dug the roots are easily worked; later they become hard and smooth.*

Right: Herb gardens are a medley of plants, from annuals to shrubs such as Bay (*Laurus nobilis*), which has leaves highly valued by cooks.

When preparing a herb garden, dig the ground deeply in winter if previously uncultivated; otherwise, to the depth of a single spade's blade. Remove all perennial weeds, and mix in garden compost or well-decomposed manure to aid moisture retention during dry periods and to provide nutrition for plants. In spring, rake the surface level.

Herb beds

Beds more than 1.5 m deep are difficult to look after, as plants at the back are difficult to reach; if a bed of this depth is backed by a hedge, it is advisable to leave a 45–60 cm wide path between the plants and screen. Hedges are gross feeders and take a great deal of food and, especially, water from the soil, making the area around them exceptionally dry and barren.

If there is a grass path or lawn along the front of a herb border, overhanging plants will eventually cause unsightly bare patches. To prevent this happening – and to let herbs trail and cascade in a natural manner – cut away the turf and put down an edging of paving slabs.

Most new herb gardens are planted in spring or early summer from container-grown plants. Before setting plants in position, plan the border on grid paper: if possible, plant herbs in clusters of three, as this quickly creates dominant displays. When the plan is complete, water both the soil and plants to encourage rapid development when planting is complete. A day or so later – when the surface of the soil is starting to become dry – use dry, sharp sand to mark on the soil the outline of each planting area.

Carefully remove each herb from its pot, then plant it firmly; make sure each plant is labelled. When planting is complete, lightly scarify the soil's surface, and thoroughly but lightly water the entire area. Repeat the watering until plants are established and growing strongly.

Cartwheel herb gardens

Growing herbs in a circular, cartwheel-shaped arrangement creates a decorative and spectacular garden feature. Even if a large cartwheel is not available, its image can be formed on a prepared site by using large, coloured pebbles to create spokes and a large hub at its centre. Alternatively, rustic poles can be used to form the spokes.

CULINARY HERBS

Popular culinary herbs include angelica, aniseed, balm, basil, bay, borage, caraway, chervil, chives, coriander, dill, fennel, hyssop, lovage, marjoram, mint, parsley, rosemary, rue, sage, savory, tarragon and thyme.

HERBS IN CONTAINERS

Tubs, pots, herb-planters, troughs, and window boxes planted with herbs on a warm, sunny patio are a visual tonic as well as a culinary blessing. Balconies can also be made more exciting with a few pots of herbs.

Large herbs such as rosemary and bay are best grown in tubs, but chervil, chives, parsley, pot marjoram, summer savory, sweet basil and thyme are ideal for planting in pots and window boxes. Mint is invasive and always best planted in a large pot.

Sage and rue can also be grown in large pots, and when they become too large transferred into a herb garden.

Keeping the soil moist is the most important part of growing plants in pots; grouping them together makes watering easier. Nevertheless, during summer, plants need to be checked several times a day to ensure the potting mixture remains moist.

Right: Cottage-garden herb gardens can be made accessible throughout the year by using stepping stones set into thyme paths.

FREEZING HERBS

Herbs retain their flavour for up to six months after freezing. Young shoots and sprigs can be frozen whole by placing them in plastic bags and then sealing. Another method is to freeze them in water. Finely chop the leaves, place in ice-cube trays, top up with bottled water and freeze. When frozen, remove the cubes and place in plastic bags, labelling each bag with the contents and date.

Small, relatively low-growing herbs, such as mint, sage and thyme suit a cartwheel display. Use a dominant plant in the centre, such as bay (*Laurus nobilis*).

Chequerboard designs

Prepare a flat area, and lay paving slabs in a chequerboard layout, so that an equal number of isolated squares of soil are created. Different herbs can then be planted in them, and by using variegated herbs as well as all-green varieties, an eye-catching display can be created. If the herbs – when young or if small – do not fill their allotted area, spread stone chippings around them; this highlights the plants, prevents the growth of weeds and keeps the soil moist.

When creating chequerboard herb gardens, use paving slabs with ribbed surfaces and in natural colours, so that they harmonize with plants. Smooth-surfaced paving slabs in bright, garish colours are not suitable.

HERBAL APHRODISIACS

Herb gardens appear natural areas for plants with aphrodisiac qualities, where native plants often jostle for space with exotic brethren.

Fennel (*right*) was known to Romans for its ability to give strength, while in the *Kama Sutra* it is claimed to aid sexual activity.

Fenugreek, indigenous to the eastern Mediterranean countries, has seeds that are claimed to act as an aphrodisiac.

Ginseng, often said to be the wonder of the world, is claimed to aid mental and physical well-being and to increase sexual potency.

Wild Marjoram, which symbolizes happiness, is said to cause relaxation through its sweet scent.

Meadowsweet, also known as Bride-

wort, has a sweet fragrance, and was earlier used as a strewing herb at wedding ceremonies.

Mint is used in Eastern countries to encourage virility, while the sixteenth-century herbalist John Parkinson suggested that Aristotle and other Greek writers said that it did much to incite sexual desire.

Myrtle has long been a part of wedding ceremonies, and in Roman times a distillation of the flowers and leaves, together with wine, was used to create a love-inciting drink.

Sea Holly, also known as Sea Holme and Sea Hulver, has roots with aphrodisiac qualities, and was earlier considered by Arabs to be an excellent restorative.

Vervain, known as Herba Veneris and Herbe Sacrée, was claimed by the Egyptians, Chinese, Persians, Celts and Romans to have love-promoting powers; it was also used by priests in sacrifices.

FLOWERS FOR HEALING

To many people, even the word 'flower' has magical qualities, conjuring thoughts of beauty, expressions of love and romance, myths and superstitions. Flowers have even been messengers of love and given their own vocabulary of sentiments. All of these qualities have an inspirational and healing nature.

Gardens are usually awash with a medley of flowers from many countries, almost to the exclusion of native types. This has been the trend for several centuries, with plant hunters from many countries going forth and returning with plants and seeds. Gardens are therefore more cosmopolitan than we may care to realize, and even in hardy annual flower beds there may be Californian Poppies, *Eschscholzia californica* (which, incidentally, encouraged the Spaniards to call the country 'The Land of Fire' and 'The Golden West'), nestling alongside Sweet Sultan, *Amberboa moschata* (earlier and still better known as *Centaurea moschata*), from the Orient, and the once ubiquitous Field Poppy, *Papaver rhoeas,* from Britain, mainland Europe and many other regions. There is a case, however, for growing groups of plants native to your own area or country, as they are not only attractive but also provide ideal homes for native birds, mammals and insects, and supply them with food.

NATIVE FLOWER GARDENS

These are formed of a mixture of plants, from grasses and hardy annuals to herbaceous perennials and bulbs. The selection of these plants must be tailored to the climate, soil type, exposure, shade, full sun and so on.

Native plants often prefer soil low in fertility; excessive nutrition encourages rank, lush growth that is vulnerable to cold weather and subject to attack by pests and diseases. If the area has been neglected for several years, dig it in winter and allow to settle by spring. Firm the surface and rake level before sowing in spring. Take care to remove perennial weeds such as docks, dandelions and horsetails.

Mixtures of native flowers are sold by many seed merchants; these are best mixed with fine, dry sand to make distribution easier.

FLOWERS FOR HOME DECORATION

A few fresh flowers in a vase indoors never fail to brighten a room, introducing an atmosphere of happiness and well-being. They are also traditional messengers of good wishes to people in hospitals.

Arranging flowers to create attractive displays is not difficult, and although aficionados of the art may lay down rules, it is really a matter of personal taste about the ones selected and how they are arranged.

Many annuals and herbaceous perennials are ideal for cutting and displaying

Facing page: The Field Poppy (*Papaver rhoeas*) was the scourge of farmers when it repeatedly grew among crops, but in a wild flower garden it creates a vivid display. Young growth, before the formation of flower buds, is considered edible and can be used to make salads.

Above centre: This delicately coloured Victorian illustration of flowers appeared in *The Language of Flowers,* one of the many books that have been published on this still intriguing subject.

117

REVERSING THE MEANING

The correct presentation of a flower was essential if its meaning was to be interpreted without confusion. If inverted and presented hanging down, the meaning was reversed. For example, a rosebud when given with its thorns and leaves intact to a lady implied 'I fear, but I hope'. And if returned upside-down to the gentlemen it meant 'You must neither fear nor hope'.

Above right: Seedheads create distinctive features in flower borders. Here, the large seedheads of the Opium Poppy, *Papaver somniferum*, are highlighted by a background of Golden Rod (*solidago*). The seedheads can be cut with long stems and used indoors to decorate rooms.

Facing page: Many flowers can be cut, gathered into bunches and hung upside down to dry. They can be used to create memorable displays for many months.

Dictamnus albus, the Gas Plant or fraxinalla, is another herbaceous perennial, with spider-like, white flowers during early and midsummer. When the pods are formed, cut the stems.

Echinops ritro, the Globe Thistle, is a plant with a similar nature, and displays steel-blue flower heads during mid- and late summer.

Iris foetidissima, variously known as Gladwyn Iris, Stinking Iris, Gladdon and Scarlet-seeded Iris, is hardy, with insignificant, purple flowers during early summer. Later, it produces attractive seed pods.

Onopordum acanthium, widely known as Scotch Thistle, Giant Thistle and Cotton Thistle, is another herbaceous perennial, with broad, silvery leaves and pale-purple, thistle-like flowers up to 5 cm wide during mid- and late summer.

The Oriental Poppy (*Papaver orientale*), a herbaceous perennial, has large, scarlet flowers during early summer, followed by seedheads that look superb when dried.

Popularly known as Chinese Lantern, Bladder Cherry, Alkekengi and Winter Cherry, *Physalis alkekengi* is a herbaceous perennial with white flowers in midsummer, following by orange fruits enclosed in papery, bright-red, lantern-like cases. Cut the stems when the lanterns show colour.

Several plants with an 'everlasting' nature are annuals – or are treated as annuals. *Limonium sinuatum* 'Azure', the Sea Lavender, is grown as a half-hardy annual and develops azure blue flowers from midsummer to autumn. There are many other varieties, in colours including yellow, orange, carmine, pink and white.

Gnaphalium 'Fairy Gold', widely known as Cudweed, is another plant that is usually grown as a half-hardy annual and develops silvery-grey leaves and double,

yellow to orange flowers during midsummer.

The Strawflower or Immortelle, *Helichrysum* 'Bright Bikini Mixed,' is a half- hardy annual, with large, daisy-like flowers in many colours from midsummer to autumn.

Bells of Ireland, *Moluccella laevis,* has a similar nature, and throughout summer bears olive to emerald-green bells. When cut and dried, they last for several years.

CREATING BUTTERFLY GARDENS

Few insects that invade our gardens are as delicate and attractive as butterflies, which, on summer days, create idyllic scenes of both tranquillity and vitality. The vibrancy and fascination they generate helps to produce a stimulating yet restful environment – and one that has healing qualities.

Buddleia, lavender, lilac and ligustrum (privet) are shrubs that attract butterflies, while achillea, Mich- aelmas Daisies, centranthus, erigeron, heleniums, scabious, *Sedum spectabile*, and Solidago (Golden Rod) are border perennials that entice them into gardens.

DRYING SEEDHEADS AND FLOWERS

Cut the stems of flowers that are to be dried just before they are fully open; make sure they have long stems. For seedheads, sever stems just when the pods change colour. Tie them into loose bunches and hang upside-down in a dry, cool or slightly warm, well-ventilated room. Leave them until all moisture has gone, but avoid drying them too rapidly.

There are many other plants to choose from such as Acanthus spinosus *(Bear's Breeches),* Anaphalis triplinervis *(Pearly Everlasting),* Cynara cardunculus *(Cardoon),* Eryngium *(Eryngo), and* Limonium latifolium *(Sea Lavender).*

bestowing garlands of laurel on victorious athletes, were giving unwritten messages of acclaim. Also, the Druids cherished the oak. However, the popularity of the meanings of flowers is mainly owed to the celebrated eighteenth-century letter-writer and society poet Lady Mary Wortley Montagu, who, in 1716, accompanied her husband to Constantinople (later Istanbul) when he was sent as the British ambassador to the court of a Turkish sultan.

The passing of messages through flowers was known in Turkey in the 1600s, and Lady Mary soon sent letters back to England which detailed the use of flowers in a language of love. She claimed that it was possible, by the use of flowers, to send messages of love and passion – as well as to quarrel – without 'inking the fingers'.

A few years later, she returned to England, giving more popularity to the use of flowers to express sentiments but, unfortunately, then quarrelling with the satirist Alexander Pope. She went to France, popularized the language of flowers and did not return for another twenty years.

The hardy annual *Celosia* 'Flamingo Feather', a Woolflower, has rose and deep-pink flowers during summer.

Craspedia globosa 'Drumsticks', usually grown as a half-hardy annual, develops silver leaves and yellow flowers during midsummer.

Above: The herbaceous Chinese Lantern, *Physolis alkekengi* creates a wealth of papery, bright red, lantern-like cases. These can be cut with long stems and used for room decoration. In warm regions it produces a delicious edible fruit and is known as the cape gooseberry.

MESSENGERS OF LOVE

Love is a healing quality, and for hundreds of years sentiments have been attributed to flowers, leaves and thorns. Flowers given by Greeks during classical times had meanings, while the Romans, when

FLOWERS FOR BUTTONHOLES

Wearing flowers in button-holes in the lapels of coats and jackets was popular for only a relatively short time, and appears to have been mainly a Victorian fashion. Up to the time of the First World War, most fashionable men in London wore a buttonhole – perhaps the most famous were the chrysanthemum of the English wit,

dramatist and poet Oscar Wilde (above), and the orchid of the Liberal politician Joseph Chamberlain.

The origins of buttonholes are not clear; a tenuous suggestion has been that Prince Albert took a flower from a bouquet of his wife, Queen Victoria, cut a slit in his tunic and inserted the flower. Another proposes that when Napoleon founded the Legion of Honour in 1802, its ribbon was red, the colour of carnations. Many men who did not receive this honour took to wearing a red carnation as a buttonhole.

There became a style, an etiquette, of wearing a buttonhole: no foliage was to be used to back it and only a red carnation was suitable. However, violets could be worn with a pink hunting coat, and a white carnation with white tie and tails.

To make sure the buttonhole remained fresh, some men wore a glass tube into which the stem was inserted. However, this innovation was known earlier in France, when at the time of the French Revolution women wore flowers in their hair.

Today, the custom of wearing a button-hole is most frequently seen at weddings; the flower is usually a white carnation backed by Asparagus Fern or Maidenhair Fern, and the stem covered in foil.

**LEFT OR
RIGHT HAND?**

*The choice of hand used to
present a flower had a
distinct meaning in the*
Language of Flowers.
*When a flower was given in
answer to a question, to offer
it with the left hand
suggested a negative, but
with the right as affirmative.*

The French took up the romanticism of flower messages, and about the middle of the 1800s many books were published in English, mainly derived from earlier works written by Mme de la Tour, who had become an acknowledged authority. Unfortunately, many of the interpretations in French books were too lusty for genteel Victorian English society, and therefore had to be omitted or toned down.

GOOD LUCK FLOWERS

Bringing luck to oneself has been a desire of Man since he first walked upright and wished to have a little help to aid physical survival and to give spiritual succour and hope, as well as good health.

Whether known as talismans, charms or amulets, these mascots – lucky stones, colours, certain numbers, flowers, jewels or animals – have became an important part in the lives of many people.

Custom and tradition suggest that for a mascot to be successful and to endow the possessor with health and happiness, it must not be obtained unjustly and, preferably, should be given by a friend and represent a token of gratitude.

Flowers are important gifts and good luck tokens, and each year are given in their millions during festivals. Here are a few good luck flowers, several with claimed benefits for lovers:

Foxgloves are lucky to grow in gardens

and are steeped in fairy folklore, a connection revealed by the dainty, bell-like flowers, earlier known as Fairy Thimbles, Fairy Caps and Fairy's Glove.

Hawthorn brings good fortune when fixed to the outside of a door, but bad luck if taken indoors.

Heather has long been given to bring good luck and health to the recipient. White heather, through its rarity, is thought to bestow more luck than the purple type.

Houseleeks have long been said to protect houses from lightning and fire; in many countries, they have been encouraged to grow on both thatched and tiled roofs.

Above left: The herbaceous Globe Thistle, *Echinops ritro*, develops upright stems topped with globular, steel-blue flower

FLEUR-DE-LIS

The Yellow Water Flag, Iris
pseudacorus *(also known as*
Yellow Flag and Water
Flag), is said to have given
inspiration and form to the
fleur-de-lis, the armorial
emblem of the kings of
France. In the sixth century,
Clovis I, the king of the
Franks, was in a battle with
his escape blocked by a river.
He noticed that in one area
the Yellow Water Iris grew
nearly across the river,
indicating its shallowness.
He escaped across the river
and in gratitude adopted the
flower as his emblem.

Lavender brings good luck and health to lovers; earlier, scented bags of it were an essential part of a bride's trousseau.

Lotus flowers, now tokens of good luck and health, were emblems of fertility in Egyptian, Chinese and Hindu mythology.

Marsh Mallows have long been considered good luck flowers for lovers; a bunch of them on a doorstep or windowsill ensures faithfulness.

Mistletoe is not without its admirers at Christmas, when Western custom dictates the exchange of kisses for festive frolickers lingering under it.

Myrtle is another flower sacred to lovers, and for many years part of bridal wreaths, when it is said to bring good luck and health.

Rosemary means 'remembrance', and is the mascot of lovers and friends; the gift of a sprig of it is said to guarantee that the recipient's thoughts concentrate on the sender.

Rue was widely used to repel germs, as well as being a charm against witchcraft, when it was said to bring good fortune.

Shamrock normally has three leaves, and Christians therefore give it religious significance associated with the Holy Trinity. The good luck powers of the four-leafed type can be traced back to the Druids; it is claimed that the possession of a four-leafed clover makes wishes come true.

FASHIONS IN FLOWERS

Throughout the centuries many flowers have become fashionable, but later to have fallen into obscurity. In mid-eighteenth century England, for example, the English daisy, *Bellis perennis,* was widely grown, and there were more than twelve varieties.

Here are a few flowers that have been popular at particular times (the dates given are only approximations):

Lotus – Indian and ancient Egypt.

Violets – Well known in Athens about 400 BC as well as in Europe (especially France) from 1790 to 1830 and, later, from 1870 to 1914.

Roses – Imperial Rome, when Cleopatra is said to have seduced Mark Anthony in a room knee-deep in roses. The development of Hybrid Tea roses started in Europe in the nineteenth century and created fresh interest in roses.

Rosemary – Involved in legends and ancient beliefs in the Middle Ages in Europe, from about 500 to 1450 AD.

Lilies – Known in Greece at least 1500 years BC.

Fritillaries – Earlier popular in Turkey, and gained enthusiastic followers in Germany during the sixteenth and seventeenth centuries.

Tulips – In the early 1600s, French women popularized tulips by pinning them to their low and rather risqué décolleté, while between 1634 and 1637 tulip mania swept Holland.

Facing page: Krishna, in Sanskrit meaning 'the black one', is one of the greatest Hindu deities and often depicted as a handsome young man playing a flute. Here, the God Krishna is seen in the rain with the sacred lotus flower, which symbolizes the sun.

STYLES IN WEDDING FLOWERS

Myrtle has long been part of bridal bouquets, especially in Mediterranean countries, and is claimed to have been part of flower arrangements in early Jewish weddings. Greek girls had bridal bouquets of roses combined with myrtle underneath their purple veils.

From before the nineteenth century myrtle was often part of English bridal flowers, and it is claimed that many bushes of this shrub later found growing by the side of a cottage door owe their existence to being grown from a cutting taken from a bouquet. The planting was always done by the bride, never the groom! At the same time, the path to the church was often strewn with rosemary, marigolds and broom.

The ritual of scattering rice – now usually confetti – over the bride and groom is intended to bring good luck. It derives from the East and is a symbol of prosperity and fruitfulness. However, in Saxon times in England, barley and wheat were used for the bride to step on.

Since the time of Charlemagne (also known as Charles the Great), about AD 800, brides throughout the Frankish Empire had rosemary in their bridal bouquets; sprigs of this fragrant shrub were also worn by ladies – usually on the bosom – as a symbol of devotion.

Orange blossom wreaths, however, originated in the East; after the religious Crusades from the eleventh to the thirteenth centuries, European brides often included it in their bouquets.

In the early 1900s in North America, it was claimed that the custom of the bride throwing a bunch of flowers to friends gathered around her – the one who caught it being the next to marry – could be traced to an earlier habit of 'flinging the bride's stocking', a wedding ritual practised from about 1600 to 1750.

125

MESSAGES IN KNOTS

Sometimes, when boxes of flowers were sent to lovers, the position of the knot in the ribbon securing the flowers had added significance. If the knot was on the left side, it expressed a message about the giver, but on the right about the recipient.

THE LANGUAGE OF BOUQUETS

Bouquets of flowers reveal more complex messages than those offered by single flowers in the *Language of Flowers*. Also, the attitudes of flowers have meanings: a flower bent towards the right signifies 'I', whereas one inclined to the left implies 'You'. This, when combined with the meaning of the flowers, makes messages more personal. For example, a red rosebud when leaning toward the left means 'You are pure and lovely', while a snowdrop bent to the right implies 'I hope'.

Leaves and, if present, thorns on stems also have meanings: leaves signify hope, while thorns signify danger. A folded ivy leaf around a bouquet means 'I have'; a laurel leaf in a similar position suggests 'I am'; a leaf of the Virginia Creeper tells 'I give'; a tendril of an ivy expresses a wish.

Examples of Victorian bouquets and the meanings of their flowers include:

Geranium (Oak-leafed type), Gillyflower and Heliotrope (with a leaf of Virginia Creeper) – 'I offer true friendship, affection and devotion.'

Monkshood, Mountain Ash and blue Violets – 'Danger is near. Be prudent. Be faithful.'

Vervain, Sweet Basil, Shepherd's Purse (wrapped in a laurel leaf) – 'I am enchanted with you. I wish you well. I offer you my all.'

Mistletoe, Hawthorn, Heliotrope (turned to the right when presented) – 'I surmount difficulties. I hope. I turn to thee.'

Red Poppies, Clematis, Harebell (bound with Virginia Creeper) – 'I offer consolation. You have mental beauty. I submit to you.'

Hyacinths – Widely grown in Turkey, but they created a near mania in Holland from 1637 to the turn of the century. They were also popular in Germany in the late nineteenth century.

Auriculas, anemones, hyacinths, tulips, ranunculus, carnations and *polyanthus* – Widely grown in England during the latter part of the nineteenth century.

Daisies – Popular in England in the mid-1700s, with many varieties, including the Double Pyed Quilled Daisy, Double Painted Lady Daisy, and Double Speckled Coxcomb Daisy.

Forget-me-nots – Popular as houseplants in France in the nineteenth century.

Dahlias – Widely grown in France in the 1830s, England in the 1840s, as well as Germany.

Fuchsia – In Berlin from 1830 to 1840.

Camellia – Popular in France from 1840 to 1860.

Mignonette – Popularized as a house-plant in Paris by the Empress Josephine in the late 1700s and early 1800s; slightly later in London.

Orchids – Popular in North America and Europe in the 1870s.

FLOWER APHRODISIACS

The range of flowers with aphrodisiac qualities is smaller than with vegetables and herbs, although it is said that almost any flower inclines the mind to beauty and love, encouraging good health and happiness. Indeed, flowers at weddings invariably encourage thoughts of romanticism.

Orange blossom, earlier popularized in bridal bouquets by the Saracens and a symbol of pre-marriage chastity, can be infused to create a tonic for nervous brides. The long, straggly roots of the Dog Violet, *Viola canina* (also known as the Heath Violet), have been claimed to aid amorous overtures. *Crème de Violette,* a syrup produced from the Sweet Violet (*Viola odorata*) and known as *Parfait Amour,* is often part of love potions.

Orchids, with the root parts of terrestrial types resembling testicles, have frequently been considered to have importance in love emotions.

Gladiolus and asphodel bulbs were earlier thought to be aphrodisiacs, while a

Facing page: Orchids, with their wide range of colours and flower shapes, have always been popular, especially during the late nineteenth century.

Below: Natural, woodland settings create areas for relaxation and contemplation in many temperate regions. This idyllic setting is in Mount Cube, Delaware.

LILIVM *flo:* ALBO
Lis Blancq
lilien ganls weis gemeine.

plateful of tulip bulbs was said to aid any young man.

In India, the Thorn Apple, *Datura alba,* has long been a medicinal plant with claimed aphrodisiac powers; the seeds when crushed were applied externally to sexual organs for aphrodisiac purposes. However, it is a poisonous plant, and even today young children die through eating half-ripe seeds.

The Winter Cherry (*Withania somnifera*) is another plant used in India as an aphrodisiac. Ayurvedic physicians believe that the root of this plant improves the sperm count, which has led to the claim that powdered root, when taken with milk or clarified butter, acts as an aphrodisiac.

FLOWERS FOR THE DEAD

Funerals have long had the dual role of helping the departed into another world and comforting the bereaved. Floral wreaths, formed of flowers and foliage plants, are said to help the dead into another world, while tombs in ancient Egypt were furnished with food to provision the soul against the risks of hunger.

Flowers were often buried with the dead, as well as carefully thrown into an open grave as a last token of love. Indeed, burials at sea usually involve casting wreaths and flowers on the water's surface.

Gardens for the dead were laid out by the Egyptians, who believed that the goddess of death, sitting under a beautiful, shade-giving tree, greeted the dead, offering water and fruits.

The ancient Greeks scattered lilies on graves; at that time these flowers were the symbol of virginity and chastity. They were said to flower on graves of innocent people who had been executed. At the same time, irises were planted on the graves of women, while periwinkle was made into wreaths for dead babies.

Rosemary gained popularity in England and parts of Europe during the seventeenth and eighteenth centuries as a symbol for remembrance. In France, it was the custom to put a sprig of rosemary in the hands of the dead, while in England, the custom of casting sprigs into graves lasted well into the nineteenth century.

Today, with a wide range of florists' flowers available almost throughout the year, it is more likely that flowers used at funerals represent the favourites of the deceased, rather than traditional types.

Facing page: Lilies have been acclaimed and cherished for many centuries. This Madonna Lily (*Lilium candidum*), earlier known as *L. albo and L. album*, was known to the Cretans between 1750 and 1600 BC.

Above left: Astrological gardens, where the sowing, planting and harvesting of crops are guided by the signs of the zodiac, are increasingly popular, and for many gardeners are the secret of success with plants and the soil.

Left: This astrological clock, formed of colour-contrasting stones, attracts attention throughout the year.

HEALING HARVESTS

*Throughout the world, vegetables, fruits, berries, nuts and several fungi are
grown or gathered as food, thereby helping to keep people healthy and fit.
Some of them have medicinal values and frequently form the bases of country
cures; others provide additional vitamins and a few are aphrodisiacs.*

MEDICINAL VEGETABLES

Beetroots, with their beautifully coloured, swollen roots, when cooked, are said to be a general curative for the head, from baldness and hair shedding to dandruff and scurf They are also claimed to be good for blisters, pustules and wheals on the skin.

Cucumbers, an essential part of summer salads (earlier known as cowcumbers), are almost entirely formed of water, but have been acclaimed for their ability to ease ulcers in the bladder. Their seeds encourage the development of urine and cleanse passages. The seeds are also said to expel tapeworms.

Kidney beans were cultivated and worshipped by the ancient Egyptians because the seeds resembled testicles. Because they were so highly valued, they were banned as food. Early medicinal uses suggest bruising and boiling the beans with garlic as a cure for coughs, while recent uses include a cure for rheumatism and an aid for urinary tract

disorders. These beans, when partially cooked, especially at low temperatures, are dangerous to eat!

Onions have many medicinal country uses, including increasing the production of sperm, while their juice, when made into a syrup, eases coughs and colds. A variation on this is roasting onions and eating them with sugar and honey. Chopped onions, when added to gin, are said to be a cure for oedema and kidney stones. More recent uses of onions include alleviating the symptoms of hay fever and rhinitis.

Even the ubiquitous potato, native to South America and introduced into Europe in the sixteenth century, has a medicinal value. Old country cures using potatoes include hot potato water for easing rheumatism and swollen areas. Another was to steep sliced but unpeeled tubers, plus unripe berries, in cold water and to apply it as a cold compress. A variation on this was used to ease and heal scalds and burns, while the mealy flour produced by boiling the tubers, when mixed with an oil, has been used to alleviate frostbite. Hot potatoes are claimed to remove corns!

Radishes, now part of summer salads, have been grown in Europe and temperate Asia for many years, and are used to encourage the flow of urine and to ease kidney stone and gravel symptoms. Also, the roots are said to be an antidote to scurvy.

Wild carrots were mentioned by the ancient Greeks for use in cooking, while in the early seventeenth century the feathery leaves featured in ladies' head-dresses. Early herbalists claimed that a

Facing page: Lovers, minstrels and music are central features of this medieval castle garden which abounds with fruit trees and flowers, while the ubiquitous daisy peppers the lawn's surface.

Above centre: Beans are grown and eaten in many parts of the world; they are annually raised from seeds that within one growing season germinate, grow and produce edible pods and seeds.

poultice made from carrot roots eases cancerous ulcers, and that the soft, ferny leaves, when coated with honey, were ideal for cleansing sores and ulcers. The roots are recommended to remove stitches in the side and as a carminative, while the seeds are said to be ideal to cure oedema and to reduce the size of swollen bellies.

THE KITCHEN GARDEN

Even the term kitchen garden has a warm, homely sound that implies some thing more than just a vegetable patch. Kitchen gardens have been known for several thousand years, producing vegetables, herbs and fruits. Some of the

earliest of these were in Peru, more than 2000 years ago, growing potatoes, sweet potatoes, peanuts, beans, squashes and fruits such as avocados and guavas. While at about the time of the birth of Christ the Roman writer Pliny the Elder described twelve or more types of cabbages and kale, eleven lettuces and many onions.

Nowadays, the art of kitchen gardening is to produce a range of food crops from a small area and often in containers on a patio or terrace. When selecting varieties of vegetables choose those that are especially tasty and crop over a long period. Unfortunately, Fl varieties tend to produce their crop over a short period,

creating a glut. Some of the older fruit varieties have greater taste appeal than many commercial types that are

GODDESS OF THE HARVEST

Ceres, the Roman goddess of food plants, was either worshipped alone or in association with the earth goddess Tellus. At an early date her cult was overlaid by that of Demeter, the goddess of grain.

Above right: Gooseberries are a popular summer fruit. They gained their name because they were earlier used to make a sauce to accompany goose. The berries also have several medicinal values, including a cure for inflammation.

Right: Vegetable plots can be just as colourful and varied as flower gardens, which is important in small gardens. Grow a medley of vegetable plants with colourful and interestingly shaped leaves, and include some climbers. Strawberries and tayberries, as well as other fruits, can be included.

and carberries, as well as feverberries and feaberries in the sixteenth century, when plague victims were recommended to eat them. Also, the juice of berries is claimed to cure inflammation, and ripe berries to reduce 'violent heat' in the stomach and liver. Earlier, the leaves were eaten to ease the effects of gravel in the kidneys and bladder.

Grapes were mentioned by Homer in the tenth century BC as a drink, while in his *Iliad* they figured as an emblem on Achilles' shield. The fruits – apart from being made into wine or vinegar – have several medicinal values and ripe grapes are claimed to increase the flow of urine and to help in the treatment of smallpox. One cure for torpid liver and sluggish biliary functions was to eat 1.5–2.75 kg of fresh grapes every day! In addition, leaves boiled with barley meal create a poultice to ease inflammation.

Plums have been grown in gardens for centuries, and their fruits are used for many culinary purposes, but they also have medicinal values when dried,

primarily selected for their appearance and keeping qualities while travelling to the market place.

MEDICINAL FRUITS

Many fruits grown in gardens have medicinal qualities, and some of them and their uses are steeped in antiquity.

Figs are rich in history. Native to Syria and Palestine, they spread to Greece and, soon after, to Asia Minor and Italy. The fruits are a staple part of many diets. They also act as a mild laxative and are part of proprietary preparations, including Syrup of Figs. Figs are also part of nasal treatments, clearing noses and soothing throats, while the soft parts of roasted fruits are formed into a poultice to treat boils and carbuncles. The milky juice is said to remove warts.

Gooseberries, which gained their name through use as a sauce to accompany goose, were earlier known as honeyblobs

GROWING ONIONS FROM SETS

Onion sets are small, partly developed bulbs which have been stored during winter ready for planting in spring. During the latter part of early spring, prepare the soil in the same way as when sowing onion seeds. Also, thoroughly water the soil a few days before planting sets.

Use a draw hoe to form drills approximately 20 mm deep and 25 cm apart.

Remove the line before setting the sets in position – if left in place, there is a chance that when the line is removed it will disturb them. Just push the sets into the soil, 10 cm apart and with their tops just showing above the soil's surface.

Birds are often troublesome, attempting to disturb the sets. Therefore, cover the rows with tunnels formed of wire netting.

CURING TOOTHACHE

Toothache has always been a debilitating problem, especially in earlier years when dental care was not as reliable, One method used to reduce pain was to soak whole cloves (Eugenia caryophyllata) in hot honey and to let the patient chew them slowly near to the aching tooth. Dried cones of the hop (Humulus lupulus) have also been used to create a sedative against toothache.

Above left: The succulent fruits of plum trees are superb in summer and are delicious when picked and eaten fresh, or prepared for a dessert. They can also be dried to create prunes, known for their laxative properties.

plums, as well as when fresh and ripe. Prunes are a laxative, while the juice on its own has similar properties and is also recommended for obesity, skin eruptions, dyspepsia and haemorrhoids.

Pomegranates have been cultivated since ancient times, both for their succulent fruits and their medicinal value. The flowers produce a red dye, and in earlier times were used as an astringent medicine to remove worms. A decoction of the bark is also said to expel worms, while the rind of the fruit checks dysentery and diarrhoea.

Pumpkins are well-known fruits, especially popular as the main ingredient in traditional Thanksgiving pies. It is, however, the seeds that have medicinal properties, and when crushed and liquidized in water they create an emulsion for expelling tapeworms.

Quinces, throughout the Middle Ages frequently seen at wedding feasts, have seeds and soft flesh that moisten the throat and assist in easing fevers and soothing throats.

The fruits of raspberries, also called Red Raspberry, European Raspberry and Framboise, are claimed to strengthen the stomach and stop vomiting. The juice of ripe fruits, when made into a syrup, prevents sickness and retching. Leaves formed into a tea are used as a gargle for sore mouths and a wash for ulcers and wounds.

Ornamental Rhubarb, *Rheum palmaturn* (also known as East Indian Rhubarb and China Rhubarb), is often grown in flower borders. It is the root part that is used medicinally, frequently as a mild purgative, although it is better known as a strengthener of the intestines. In small doses it checks diarrhoea.

Garden Rhubarb, *Rheum rhaponticum* (also known as Culinary Rhubarb, Bastard Rhubarb and Sweet Round-leafed Dock), has a medicinal value. Its roots form a mild purgative and strengthen the stomach; it is also good against venomous bites. The leaves, by the way, are poisonous and should not be eaten!

MEDICINAL BERRIES AND NUTS

Botanically, berries are forms of fruit, and for that reason could have been featured with those on previous pages. However, most of the fruits mentioned previously are cultivated types; those discussed here are a medley of types found in shrub borders, hedgerows, old gardens or just as part of the landscape.

The fruits of Black Mulberry, *Morus nigra* (also known as the Common Mulberry), were well known to early Greek and Roman writers, who acclaimed their inclusion in feasts. In addition, the juice of the leaves was said to be good against bites of serpents. Medicinally, ripe berries are a laxative, while their juice, when made into a syrup, helps to ease and cure sores in the throat and mouth. A decoction of the bark and leaves is

MYSTERIOUS ELDER

As well as offering a wealth of medicinal curatives, this deciduous European shrub, botanically known as Sambucus nigra, is steeped in superstition. During the 1600s, it was believed that elder leaves fixed to doors and windows on the last day of April would prevent the entry of witches. Russians believed elder would drive away evil spirits. In Europe it was customary to plant elder to ward off evil, and to cut down an established elder was certain to incur bad luck.

Right: A variety of squashes, including pumpkins, are well known and form parts of traditional meals, especially at Thanksgiving. They were grown by Native Americans some 2000 years before Christopher Coloumbus chanced upon their shores.

ORGANIC VEGETABLE GARDENING

POOR MAN'S MEAT

Aubergines have been known in the Middle East as 'poor man's meat' and 'poor man's caviar'. They have also been called Mad Apples and Apples of Sodom because it was thought that anyone eating them would go mad or suffer from epilepsy.

Increasingly, organically grown vegetables are available in shops, but even these do not compare with fresh, healthy, home-grown vegetables. Soil fertility is important and the regular composting of vegetable waste from kitchens and gardens is essential. Decomposed animal manures can be dug into the soil during winter, or used as a mulch, while 'green manure' crops improve the soil's structure and provide nutrients. These are crops such as mustard, fenugreek and clover that are grown on a piece of land that is 'resting' and dug into the soil before they develop seeds. It is an excellent way to improve soil when manure is not available.

claimed to ease toothache, while the leaves help to staunch bleeding.

Buckthorn, *Rhamnus catharticus,* a deciduous shrub or small tree, bears black berries that produce a juice used as a laxative. Also, bruised leaves placed on wounds reputedly stop bleeding.

Butcher's Broom, *Ruscus aculeatus* (also known as Knee Holly, Box Holly, and Jew's Myrtle), is a shrubby evergreen with pretty cherry-sized, sealing-wax-red berries; when the leaves are formed into a poultice, they help to heal broken bones.

Common Juniper, *Juniperus communis,* a large, evergreen conifer, develops berrylike fruits that remain green for about a year, then turn blue-black with a gray bloom. The berries are used in the preparation of some gins, but they also have medicinal values and are useful for treating oedema, expelling air, coughs, stomach pains, shortness of breath and rupture cramps. It is also claimed that they improve eyesight.

Dog Rose, *Rosa canina* (also knows as Brier Rose, Briar Rose, Dog Brier, and, much earlier, Hep Tree), is a prickly, deciduous shrub that flowers in late spring and early summer, later producing red seed cases known as hips or heps. As well as providing vitamin C, their medicinal qualities include alleviating dysentery and diarrhoea and easing sore throats, coughs and spitting blood, In addition, the pulp of the hips, when dried and powdered, has been used to ease colic and to break up kidney stones.

Eglantine, *Rosa rubiginosa* (earlier known as *Rosa eglanteria* and commonly as Sweet Brier and Sweet Briar), bears orange-scarlet hips, sometimes referred to as spongy apples, and earlier used for many medicinal purposes. These range from encouraging hair to grow on heads to relieving colic and dispelling worms, A conserve formed from the hips was said to strengthen the kidneys, while the roots counteracted venomous bites.

Elder, *Sambucus nigra* (frequently called the European Elder, Black Elder, Bour Tree and Pipe Tree), has long been part of folklore as an emblem of sorrow and death. The berries, when made into a wine, were recommended to ease rheumatic pains, sciatica and other forms of neuralgia. Earlier, a decoction of young leaves, when sprinkled over plants, is said to have kept off greenfly and caterpillars, while the Romans used elderberry juice as an effective hair-dye.

Mistletoe, *Viscum album,* is a somewhat woody, parasitic, evergreen plant often seen growing on branches of apple trees in gardens, but also on ash, hazel,

Right: This complex illustration appeared in *The Gardener's Labyrinth* about 1577 by Thomas Hill. The top part shows vines being trained and pruned, with turf seats in the foreground. The lower part reveals dibbers being used to put plants into raised beds.

REMOVING WARTS

Country cures for warts are varied and fascinating, ranging from handshakes by 'wart charmers' to notches cut in an elder stick (to match the number of warts to be removed), then buried. As the elder decays, the warts should disappear.

In North America, the milk-like juice of milkweed (*Asclepias, right*) has been used as a charm lotion to remove warts, while in Britain and the rest of Europe, more reliance was put on the juice of Greater Celandine.

Slightly more mystical ways include wrapping up apples, green sloes or beanpods and placing the parcel at a crossroad; whoever picks up the parcel is supposed to acquire the warts.

Ash trees were also used in wart transference; the patient visited an ash tree, and each wart was pricked with a new pin which was then pushed into the bark, accompanied by the chant:

Ashen tree, Ashen tree,
Pray buy these warts off me.

maple, lime and hawthorn trees. The whitish berries, borne in clusters at stem joints, yield a sticky substance sometimes called bird-lime and claimed to ripen tumours and swellings. More recently, homoeopathic remedies prepared from mistletoe have been used in the treatment of cancer.

Sloe Bush, *Prunus spinosa* (also known as Blackthorn), is a spiny, deciduous tree or shrub with large, marble-like, blue-black fruits known as sloes and resembling damsons. It is claimed that the sloes, when made into a mouthwash, help to strengthen loose teeth. The bark, when powdered, cures agues, while an infusion of flowers is excellent for easing colic.

Sweet Chestnut, *Castanea sativa* (also known as Jupiter's Nut and Husked Nut), is a large, deciduous tree producing catkin-like flowers in midsummer,

followed by reddish-brown nuts. The nuts had several medicinal uses and were reputed to thicken the blood. The dried kernels were beaten into a powder and mixed with honey to form a cure for coughs and spitting blood.

The walnut, *Juglans nigra* (also known as the Black Walnut), has nuts that, when unripe, are claimed to have worm-destroying qualities. Together with honey, salt and onions, the leaves have been used to combat dog bites and sore throats. More recently, the powdered bark has been used as a laxative.

VEGETABLES, FRUITS, NUTS AND FUNGI AS APHRODISIACS

Seduction must be one of the oldest human activities, and making it easier and more predictable has long been the pursuit of lovers. One means of achieving this is by the use of aphrodisiacs, which stimulate sexual desire. Hard-boiled eggs, stout (dark ale) and oysters are all held to initiate sexual desire, as well as many widely known vegetables, mushrooms, fruits and nuts.

CABBAGE TREE

Widely grown as a houseplant in temperate climates, the Cabbage Tree, *Cordyline australis*, is native to New Zealand, where it is known as *ti kauko* and *whanake*, and provides both food and medicines. An infusion of leaves creates a remedy for dysentery and diarrhoea, while rubbed and softened leaves are applied as an ointment to sores, cuts and cracks in skin.

When the eighteenth-century British explorer and navigator James Cook and his crew landed in New Zealand, they ate the boiled, blanched inner leaves and hearts.

Above left When tomatoes were introduced into Europe from South America they were known as love-apples and it was claimed that they incited sexual passion.

Far left: Mistletoe is a well-known parasite of some trees, including the apple. It is steeped in legends and was used by the Druids in their sacrificial ceremonies. It is said to have been given to the god of love, who announced that anyone passing beneath it must be given a kiss — a tradition that continues to this day.

'Frisky' vegetables

Vegetables with claimed aphrodisiac qualities include radishes, parsnips, asparagus, artichokes, tomatoes (earlier known as love-apples), leeks, celery, onions, shallots, broad beans, peas and leeks. The range is so wide that its validity is often its question. However, so renowned are a few of these vegetables in literature that claims for their sexual potency could be accurate. For example, of the ordinary culinary asparagus, *Asparagus officinalis,* it has been said that it 'manifestly provoketh Venus', while in the sixteenth century it was written in *The Perfumed Garden* that asparagus 'with yolk of egg fried in fat, camel's milk and honey causes the virile member to be alert, night and day'.

Of artichokes it is said:

> Artichokes! Artichokes!
> Heats the body and the spirit,
> Heats the genitals.

While of the shallot it is reported:

> If envious age relax the nuptial knot,
> Thy food be scallions and thy feast shallot.

An old English ballad reveals the potency of beans, saying:

> My love hung limp beneath the leaf,
> (O bitter, bitter shame!)
> My heavy heart was full of grief,
> Until my lady came.
>
> She brought a tasty dish to me,
> (O swollen pod and springing seed!)
> My love spray out right eagerly,
> To serve me in my need.

Fun-giving fungi

Truffles and a few other fungi are claimed to have sexual powers. These include the Stinkhorn or Wood-witch, *Phallus impudicus,* which was highly prized in the Far East because of its phallic appearance and development from an egglike sac.

The ordinary mushroom, widely used in cookery, is also said to be an aphrodisiac, but for this purpose it is claimed

Below: Globe Artichokes are said to create thoughts of love in those who eat them. It is a decorative vegetable well worth planting in a flower border.

CURING RHEUMATISM IN NORTH AMERICA

The North American Poke Weed, *Phytolacca americana* (also known as Poke Root, Pokeberry, Stoke, Gargot and Pigeon Berry), gains its name from the Indian *pocan,* meaning a plant that yields a red dye. This comes from the berries, the juice of which the natives of Virginia drank as a cure for rheumatism. Also, the roots, when cleaned and roasted, reduced inflammation of joints. An alternative was to boil and mash the roots to produce a warm poultice.

that it has to be pulled from the ground, rather than cut. However, it is the truffle that usually claims most importance as an invitation to love. (Incidentally, during earlier centuries the humble potato was acclaimed for its sexual powers, but this may have been because when first discovered in South America it was called the Floury Truffle.)

INDIAN APHRODISIACS

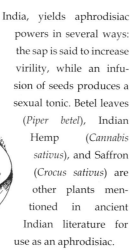

Indian literature abounds in advice about using aphrodisiacs. *Asparagus racemosus* is used in Ayurvedic medicine as an aphrodisiac; a translation of its Sanskrit name is 'many-heired', and it has been shown that its succulent tubers increase the male sperm count. The banyan, *Ficus bengolensis*, revered in India, yields aphrodisiac powers in several ways: the sap is said to increase virility, while an infusion of seeds produces a sexual tonic. Betel leaves (*Piper betel*), Indian Hemp (*Cannabis sativus*), and Saffron (*Crocus sativus*) are other plants mentioned in ancient Indian literature for use as an aphrodisiac.

Nuts for potency

Many nuts are said to have aphrodisiac qualities, including the chestnut which, in the sixteenth century, was said to incite Venus. Hazelnuts have long been acclaimed in curing male impotency, and earlier, a Latin medical book suggested that the nuts when mixed with satyrion (a range of tuberous-rooted orchids) enabled 'a man to satisfy all the desires of his wife'.

Almonds and walnuts, as well as the stones in peaches and apricots, are claimed to enrich one's sex life. Pistachios were prized by the Queen of Sheba, as they were said to 'awaken desire'.

The potency of fruit

Figs, pomegranates and bananas are fruits with aphrodisiac qualities. The pomegranate is one of the oldest Semitic symbols of life, signifying fertility and abundance. These fruits were served at marriage banquets in ancient Assyria as a symbol of love and fecundity, while at Oriental weddings the seeds of pomegranates were offered to guests. When the Moors conquered Spain in the eighth century, they introduced pomegranates into the Iberian peninsula, and the fruit became the emblem of Granada. When the French invented an explosive shell that scatters metal over a wide area they called it a 'grenade', as it resembled the seed-scattering nature of pomegranates. Regiments using these weapons were called grenadiers.

Left: The aubergines in this fifteenth century illustration from *Ortus Sanitatis* (The Garden of Health) appear to have excited the man, much to the consternation of the lady on the right who is acting as chaperone to the couple. However, this tropical Asian plant is not now noted for its ability to induce passion.

BIBLIOGRAPHY

COLOUR

Gertrude Jekyll, *Colour Schemes for the Flower Garden*, Country Life Books

Jane Lyle, *Body Language*, Reed International Books

David Squire, *Colour In Your Garden*, Salamander Books

FLORAS AND PLANT REFERENCE BOOKS

W. J. Bean, *Trees and Shrubs Hardy in the British Isles*, John Murray

Clapham, Tutin & Warburg, *Flora of the British Isles*, Cambridge University Press

James Grier, *History of Pharmacy*, The Pharmaceutical Press

Mark Griffiths (ed.), *Index of Garden Plants*, Macmillan Press

R. C. Wren, *Potter's New Cyclopaedia of Botanical Drugs and Preparations*, Health Science Press

Robert Zander, *Zander – Handwörterbuch der Pflanzennamen*, Verlag Eugen Ulmer, Stuttgart

GENERAL DICTIONARIES AND ENCYCLOPAEDIAS

Beeton's Dictionary of Universal Biography, Ward, Lock

Encyclopaedia Britannica (US edn), Encyclopaedia Britannica, Inc.

GENERAL GARDENING BOOKS

Miles Hadfield, *A History of British Gardening*, Spring Books

Geoffrey & Susan Jellicoe, Patrick Goode & Michael Lancaster, *The Oxford Companion to Gardens*, Oxford University Press

Reader's Digest Encyclopaedia of Garden Plants and Flowers, Reader's Digest Association

FOLKLORE AND HISTORY

Margaret Baker, *Folklore and Customs of Rural England*, David & Charles

Lindesey Brine, *The Ancient Earthworks and Temples of the American Indians*, Oracle Publishing

Charlotte Sophia Butte, *The Handbook of Folklore*, Senate (Studio Editions)

Chivalry – The Path of Love, Aquarium Press (HarperCollins)

Jean Harrowven, *Origins of Rhymes, Songs and Sayings*, Kaye & Ward

Christina Hole, *British Folk Customs*, Book Club Associates

T. Sharper Knowlson, *The Origins of Popular Superstitions and Customs*, Senate (Studio Editions)

Ernst & Johanna Lehner, *Folklore and Odysseys of Food and Medicinal Plants*, Harrap

Donald A. Mackenzie, *Ancient Mao in Britain*, Senate (Studio Editions)

Alexander Porteous, *The Lore of the Forest*, Senate (Studio Editions)

Elizabeth Villiers, *The Good Luck Book*, Senate (Studio Editions)

HERBALS

Nicholas Culpeper, *Culpeper's Colour Herbal*, Guild Publishing

Gerard's Herbal (reprint), Studio Editions

M. Grieve, edited and introduced by C. F. Leyel, *A Modern Herbal*, Jonathan Cape/Savvas Publishing

LANGUAGE OF FLOWERS

Lesley Gordon, *Language of Flowers*, Grange Books

Claire Powell, *The Meaning of Flowers*, Jupiter Books

Anne Pratt & Thomas Miller, *The Language of Flowers*, Simpkin, Marshall, Hamilton, Kent & Co.

The Language of Flowers, Ward Lock and Co.

MEDICINAL, COSMETIC AND APHRODISIAC USES OF PLANTS

Andrew Allen, *A Dictionary of Sussex Folk Medicine*, Countryside Books

Stefan Ball, *Flower Remedies – A Complete Guide to Dr. Bach's Natural Healing System*, Blitz Editions/Bookmart

Roberto Chiej, *Medicinal Plants*, Orbis (Macdonald)

Charles Connell, *Aphrodisiacs in Your Garden*, Arthur Barker

Ernst & Johanna Lehner, *Folklore and Odysseys of Food and Medicinal Plants*, Harrap

John Liggett, *The Human Face*, Constable

Christina Macdonald, *Medicines of the Maori*, William Collins

Nostradamus, edited by Knot Boeser, *The Elixirs of Nostradamus*, Bloomsbury Publishing

Naveen Patnaik, *The Garden of Life*, Aquarian Press (HarperCollins)

Jenny Plucknett (ed.) *Essential Aromatherapy*, Paragon Book Service

Penny Rich, *Practical Aromatherapy*, Paragon Book Service

Dr Andrew Stanway, *Alternative Medicine*, Bloomsbury Books

Nora Weeks & Victor Bullen, *The Bach Flower Remedies*, C. W. Daniel Co.

Ian White, *Australian Bush Flower Essences*, Findhorn Press

NORTH AMERICAN PLANTS

Margaret Armstrong, *Western Wild Flowers*, G. P. Putnam's Sons

C. Frank Brockman, *Trees of North America*, Golden Press

Ellwood S. &J. George Harrar, *Guide to Southern Trees*, Dover Publications, Inc.

Louise & James Bush-Brown, *America's Garden Book*, Charles Scribner's Sons

Canadian Department of Resources and Development – Forestry Branch, *Native Trees of Canada*, King's Printer and Controller of Stationery

Bernard McMahon, *McMahon's American Gardener*, Funk & Wagnalls

F. Schuyler Mathews, *Field Book of American Trees and Shrubs*, G. P. Putnam's Sons

F. Schuyler Mathews, *Field Book of American Wild Flowers*, G. P. Putnam's Sons

Staff of the Liberty *Hyde Bailey Hortorium*, Hortus Third, Macmillan Publishing

PLANTS

Tom Carter, *The Victorian Garden*, Bracken Books

Alice M. Coats, *Flowers and their Histories*, Holton Press

Alice M. Coats, *Garden Shrubs and their Histories*, Vista Books

Alice M. Coats, *The Quest for Plants*, Studio Vista

Richard Gorer, *The Growth of Gardens*, Faber & Faber

Victor Hehn, edited by James Steven Stallybrass, *Wanderings of Plants and Animals*, Swan Sonnenschein & Co.

G. Henslow, *The Uses of British Plants*, Lovell Reeve & Co.

John Hutchinson & Ronald Melville, *The Story of Plants*, Waverley Book Co.

John R. Jackson, *Commercial Botany of the Nineteenth Century*, Cassell

A. H. Lawson, *Bamboos*, Faber & Faber

A. D. & Helen Livingston, *Guide to Edible Plants and Animals*, Wordsworth Editions

H. E. Macmillan, *Tropical Planting and Gardening*, Macmillan

David Squire, *Victorian Cottage Gardens*, Colour Library Books

Gabriele Tergit, *Flowers Through the Ages*, Oswald Wolff

George Usher, *A Dictionary of Plants Used by Man*, Constable

POISONOUS PLANTS

Harry L. Arnold, *Poisonous Plants of Hawaii*, Charles E. Tuttle

A. Bernhard-Smith, *Poisonous Plants of All Countries*, Bailliere, Tindall & Cox

A. A. Forsyth, *British Poisonous Plants*, Her Majesty's Stationery Office

SCENTED PLANTS

Roy Genders, *Scented Flora of the World*, Robert Hale

Barbara Milo Ohrbach, *The Scented Room*, Clarkson N. Potter, Inc. Publishers

David Squire, *The Scented Garden*, Salamander Books

SOIL, ECOLOGY AND THE LANDSCAPE

Rachel Carson, *Silent Spring*, Hamish Hamilton

Sir A. D. Hall, *The Soil*, John Murray

Robert L. Rudd, *Pesticides and the Living Landscape*, Faber & Faber

Sir George Stapledon, *Human Ecology*, Faber & Faber

David Squire, *The Practical Gardener*, Salamander Books

Philip Wright, *Old Farm Implements*, A. & C. Black

INDEX